Collins *practical gardener*

CONSERVATORY & GREENHOUSE GARDENING

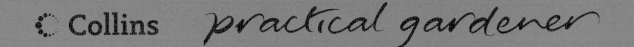

CONSERVATORY & GREENHOUSE GARDENING

LIA LEENDERTZ

First published in 2005 by HarperCollins*Publishers*

77–85 Fulham Palace Road, London, W6 8JB

The Collins website address is:

www.collins.co.uk

Text by Lia Leendertz; copyright © HarperCollins*Publishers*

Artworks and design © HarperCollins*Publishers*

The majority of photographs in this book were taken by
Tim Sandall. A number of other images were supplied
by David Sarton

Cover photography by Tim Sandall

Photographic props: Coolings Nurseries, Rushmore Hill,
Knockholt, Kent, TN14 7NN, www.coolings.co.uk

Design and editorial: Focus Publishing, Sevenoaks, Kent

Project editor: Guy Croton

Editor: Vanessa Townsend

Project co-ordinator: Caroline Watson

Design & illustration: David Etherington

For HarperCollins

Senior managing editor: Angela Newton

Editor: Alastair Laing

Assistant editor: Lisa John

Design manager: Luke Griffin

Production: Chris Gurney

A CIP catalogue record for this book is available from the
British Library

ISBN 0-00-718400-X

Colour reproduction by Colourscan

Printed and bound in Great Britain by The Bath Press Ltd

Contents

Introduction

Greenhouses or conservatories provide a half way point where houseplants flourish in higher light levels than those indoors and tender plants bloom in higher temperatures to those outside. Once you have begun gardening under glass, you will find that you can grow an increased range of plants and will have trouble squeezing them all in.

As well as giving you the opportunity to increase the variety of plants you grow under glass, a greenhouse or conservatory quickly becomes an indispensable tool for the rest of the garden. The protection afforded from the elements means that the environment can be easily manipulated and controlled, making it perfect for raising plants from cuttings and seeds, growing on bulbs and overwintering half-hardy plants.

Conservatories are usually attached to the back of the house, taking on the function of an extra room. Because of this they are often kept warm, increasing the variety of plants open to you. They are fairly expensive structures to erect but once they are up and running they are the perfect place to grow and show off some horticultural beauties. A greenhouse is a far more utilitarian beast. They are usually tucked away towards the bottom of the garden, and as such are more difficult to heat and keep warm. They often get used for more practical gardening, but can equally be made into a place of beauty, filled with ornamental plants.

Whether you are thinking of buying a greenhouse or conservatory, or have inherited one on moving into a new house, think about what you want to get out of the space and how best to set it up. The first section of this book will help you to do this. At the same time, you will find it helpful to think about the kinds of plants you would like to grow, and the sort of conditions they will require. The A–Z of ornamental plants, followed by a selection of edible plants that thrive under glass, will give you some ideas and all the information you need to keep these plants growing well and producing beautiful flowers, foliage or fruits.

All sorts of exotic plants and fruit trees can be grown in a conservatory or greenhouse environment

How to Use This Book

This book is divided into three parts. The opening chapters guide you from the outset of choosing a conservatory and greenhouse, through the planning stages of what you need to maintain the environment, and finally, general care of your plants. A comprehensive plant directory follows, with individual entries on over 130 of the most commonly available indoor house plants, including edible plants. These are listed in alphabetical order in separate chapters devoted to plants suitable for a conservatory or greenhouse, and edible plants. The final section of the book covers plant problems. Troubleshooting pages allow you to diagnose the likely cause of any problems, and a directory of pests and diseases offers advice on how to solve them.

latin name of the plant genus, followed by its **common name**

detailed descriptions give specific advice on care for each plant, including pruning and pests and diseases

alphabetical tabs on the side of the page, colour-coded to help you quickly find the plant you want

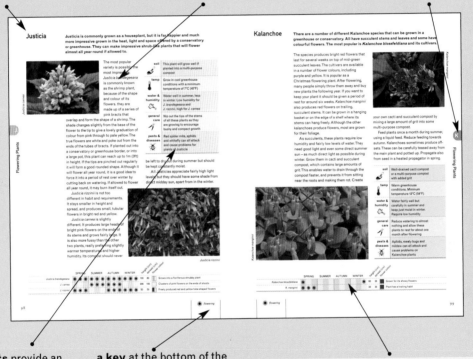

care charts provide an at-a-glance summary of the plant's specific needs (N.B. Where more than one genus appear on the page, the chart may cater for both plants)

a key at the bottom of the page explains what each symbol means

variety charts list recommended varieties for most genera of conservatory and greenhouse plants that feature more than one variety. These display key information to help you choose your ideal plant, showing:

• when (or if) the plant is in flower during the year
• when interesting nuts, berries or other fruit appear
• the height and spread after optimum growth
• the principal colour of the flowers (or foliage)
• additional comments from the author

Buying and Building a Greenhouse or Conservatory

Conservatories are often built in size and shape according to customer choice. With greenhouses, there are several different shapes available, each with its advantages and disadvantages.

Choosing a greenhouse or conservatory

Shape

The most commonly seen greenhouse is the **barn-** or **span-roof** type. These have vertical sides, which provide the maximum growing space for tall-growing plants. They can be completely glazed or have base walls on some or all sides. Base walls usually only reach up to about 1m (3ft) and can be built from wood, brick or concrete. They reduce the amount of light that the greenhouse receives, but help to retain heat. A combination of full glazing on some walls and base walls on others allows you to grow plants that need full light on one side of the greenhouse and to put up benches on the other, under which you can grow shade loving plants.

A **lean-to** uses a house wall or other wall as its fourth side. This can be useful for cutting down on heating bills,

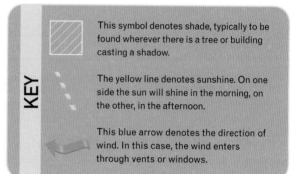

KEY

This symbol denotes shade, typically to be found wherever there is a tree or building casting a shadow.

The yellow line denotes sunshine. On one side the sun will shine in the morning, on the other, in the afternoon.

This blue arrow denotes the direction of wind. In this case, the wind enters through vents or windows.

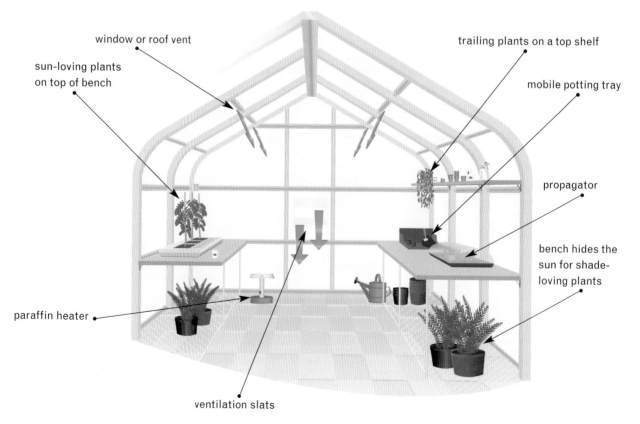

window or roof vent

sun-loving plants on top of bench

trailing plants on a top shelf

mobile potting tray

propagator

bench hides the sun for shade-loving plants

paraffin heater

ventilation slats

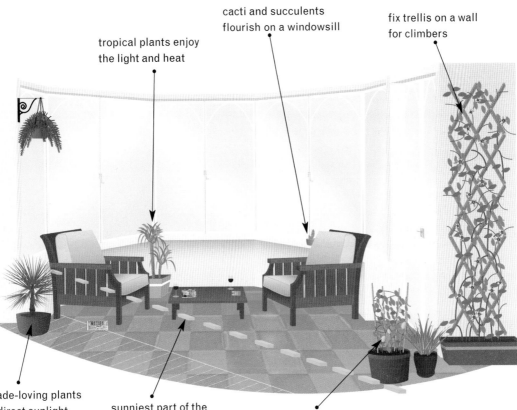

tropical plants enjoy
the light and heat

cacti and succulents
flourish on a windowsill

fix trellis on a wall
for climbers

put shade-loving plants
out of direct sunlight

sunniest part of the
conservatory

fruit trees need as much sun
and heat as possible

as house walls will give out some heat. South- or west-facing walls will also absorb heat from the sun and release it at night. Lean-tos often also have base walls on all three sides. This is particularly useful for growing vines or other climbers as a strong framework can be wired up to the house wall.

Dutch light houses are always fully glazed. Their walls lean inwards slightly to catch the most sun. These are the brightest of all greenhouses and are good for growing real sun-loving plants. However, they can be difficult to heat.

There are a number of attractive modern designs now available that bring greenhouses firmly into the 21st century. Most attractive among these is the **geodesic dome-style house**. These are attractive features to add to the garden, making it look like a miniature Eden Project. Although they look great, they are perhaps not the most practical of greenhouses. Their curved sides cut down dramatically on growing space for taller plants, and it is hard to put in any benches without ruining its good looks. However, as an attractive structure within which to provide a display of ornamental plants, they are perfect.

Conservatories are also available in many various shapes, but the major differences are mostly in style and ornamentation. This is obviously a matter of personal choice. However, do bear in mind the amount of heat that will be lost through fully glazed walls and consider going for a style with a base wall on some or all sides.

Size

The main rule when choosing a size is to go for as large as is practical. Small greenhouses always fill up with plants and are not necessarily easier to heat. Small spaces heat up quickly, but then lose heat fast. They can quickly become too hot in warm weather. A larger space will have a more even temperature. However, if you only have a small outdoor space, you should make sure that the greenhouse does not take over the whole garden.

When choosing a conservatory, consider how the house will look when it is completed. As well as planning for the amount of plants you want to grow, think about what other features you would like and take time to consider how much space benches, dining tables and chairs will take up.

Materials

Once you have decided upon the style and size of your greenhouse or conservatory, the next thing to consider is what materials you want the framework to be made out of. The main choice for greenhouses is between wood and metal.

Wood Wood is far more attractive and better at retaining heat, but is also more expensive. Cedar wood is the most commonly used hardwood. It does have a natural resistance to rotting but will still need some maintenance to keep it in good shape. Cheaper softwoods rot far more quickly and will need annual treatment. Check that they have been treated with a preservative before you buy.

Aluminium Metal greenhouses are usually made from aluminium. It is cheap, lightweight and requires a minimum of maintenance once set up. It is also stronger than wood, so the bars are thinner than those used in wood greenhouses, meaning that more light is allowed through. Glazing is often held in place by clips, so broken panes are easy to replace. However, it is less attractive and greenhouses built from it lose heat more quickly than those built from wood.

UPVC UPVC is most often used for conservatories but can also be used for greenhouses. It is fairly expensive, and not to everyone's taste, however it is easy to look after and requires no major maintenance once the greenhouse is built. Glazing bars will usually be fairly thick and so will reduce the amount of light that gets in.

Base wall If you are considering a base wall, you will need to think about which materials to use. A base wall is

TIP

If you prefer the more aesthetically pleasing sight of a wood-framed greenhouse, then softwood is a cheaper option. But beware, these greenhouses have serious problems with warping and need frequent maintenance.

usually built to about 1m (3ft) in height and any glazing starts above that point. Although they cut down on light, they are useful in retaining heat. They are constructed from brick or wood. Wood for base walls will generally be supplied as part of the greenhouse kit. Brick is the more common material used for base walls of conservatories, although it can be used for greenhouses too, and will make them more solid and permanent.

Glazing

There are various materials that can be used to glaze greenhouses and conservatories.

Glass Glass is the most popular as it retains heat well and lets in lots of light. It does not degrade over time in sunlight, as plastic does, so is a good long-term choice. Glass can also be painted with shading paint, which will wash off without affecting the quality of the glass. Horticultural glass is thick and high quality, and is often used in greenhouses. However, it breaks into long, highly dangerous splinters. Toughened glass is designed to break like a car windscreen, shattering into lots of small pieces. While most greenhouses will now have toughened or safety glass fitted as standard, check this is the case when buying.

Acrylic Sheets of acrylic are easy to work with and let through a fair amount of light, but will degrade over time in

Conservatories should be double glazed

the sun and over the years will become gradually more opaque. This can seriously affect the growth rate of plants and so acrylic panes will need replacing once they reach this stage.

Conservatory-specific In a conservatory consider fitting double glazing. This will help to keep the conservatory at a constant temperature so that it is comfortable for people and plants. The usual roofing material for conservatories is twin-wall polycarbonate. This is light and safe. It lets plenty of light through while gently diffusing it, making it perfect for softening harsh, midday sun.

Fittings and finishes

There are a few extras to check before purchasing a greenhouse or conservatory.

Ventilation Check that there are a number of windows or vents that can be easily reached and opened. This will be essential for maintaining good ventilation on hot days, when soaring temperatures and stuffy air can suffocate and scorch plants. Check that there is at least one ventilator in the roof, two or more if possible. You may be able to specify more when ordering. Although this may cost a little extra, it is well worth spending the money. Other windows should be lower down in the walls. This allows for a complete circulation of air when all are opened. Another option that is worth spending money on is an automatic ventilator. This should have a sensor that will push the vent open if the temperature rises above a

certain point and pull it closed when it drops. They are invaluable for the times when there is nobody around to monitor the temperature within the greenhouse.

Doors Look carefully at the type of door fitted to your greenhouse. The choice is between sliding and hinged doors. Sliding doors are useful as they can be left open for ventilation on particularly hot days. However, they have moving parts that are more likely to break down than those in hinged doors. Hinged doors can slam shut in winds, leading to breakages.

Drainage A small gutter at the base of sloping roofs is useful. Rain dripping straight down from roofs can form large puddles and make the area around the base of a greenhouse soggy. You can use guttering to channel rainwater into a water butt for the garden or greenhouse. Make sure the water butt is well sealed to prevent debris from getting in. Use as soon as possible to prevent fungi or any diseases building up; clean the water butt regularly. Do not use the water on any seedlings or young plants.

Always have a number of windows included...

... or at the very least, ventilation slats fitted

TIP Manufacturers generally supply the correct number of roof vents with their models. Extra roof vents do not necessarily increase the air flow in an average-size greenhouse – only adding vents lower down in the side or ends will do this.

Where to buy

Once you have thought about the type and size of greenhouse or conservatory you would like, you need to decide where you will buy yours. Conservatory companies will be able to provide you with brochures showing what is available, but it is a good idea to visit some actual conservatories to get a really good feel for the differences in size, shape and finish. Many larger garden centres have displays of conservatories and greenhouses on site, and this will give you a chance to spend time looking around them.

Alternatively, conservatory or greenhouse companies may have showrooms that you can visit. You can find contact details for these companies in your local *Yellow Pages* or in advertisements in gardening magazines.

When visiting a showroom, check how well doors and windows fit, and how easily they open and close. You should be able to move around the structure comfortably, without having to bend down or squeeze through doors.

Finally, find out if the company can provide local references and follow them up. Check if any guarantees are offered in the event of any problems with the structure.

Siting and erecting

Where to site

Conservatories are usually attached to the back of the house and so there is generally little room for discussion about their siting. However, bear the general principles of siting a greenhouse in mind when planning exactly where to put your conservatory. Where you put your greenhouse will have a bearing on how well plants will grow in it and how easy it is to look after.

Shade There are several areas that should be avoided. An obvious one is in shade – there is little point in investing in a greenhouse if you then place it where it will not get the benefit of full light. Although there are times of the year, most notably mid-summer, when shade is desirable in a greenhouse, it is far better to be able to control this and put your own shading in place than to have to put up with

TIP

When siting a greenhouse, bear in mind not only the shade from the trees in your garden, but from those in your neighbour's garden too. Look whether your or your neighbour's house cast shadows across your garden and at what time of day.

Larger garden centres often display greenhouses on site

year-round shade from a large tree or wall. In winter nearly all plants will want the maximum sunlight available. Take care near large fruit trees, as falling apples or pears can actually break panes of glass, and near evergreens, as they cast shade year round. Other trees will drop leaves that will make the glass dirty and may drop branches.

Depressions Marked depressions in the ground are also bad places to site greenhouses as they are more likely than other areas to accumulate frost or to be damp. Cold air sinks and frost pockets are formed in areas at the bottom of slopes that do not have an outlet through which the cold air can escape. Placing a greenhouse in one of these areas

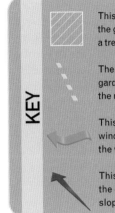

PLANNING PERMISSION

You are unlikely to need to apply for planning permission for most conservatories or greenhouses. A conservatory is classed as a building that has more than 75 per cent of the roof and more then 50 per cent of the walls made from translucent material. As such it is not classed as a 'habitable room' and so is not subject to building regulations approval. If your structure is particularly large, for instance if the floor area exceeds 30sq m (33sq yd), if it takes up more than half of the garden or if its roof exceeds the height of your current roof, you will need to look into obtaining permission. For greenhouses, no planning permission or building regulations approval is required as long as the structure meets the following conditions: it should not take up more than half of the garden; it should be less than 3m (10ft) in height with a flat roof or 4m (13ft) in height with a ridged roof; no part of the house should extend beyond a wall of the house that faces the road; and it should only used by those that occupy the house.

will be counterproductive and you will have to spend more money on fuel to keep it frost-free than you would if it were sited elsewhere.

Wind Do not to place your greenhouse in a windy area. Walk around your garden to find out where its windy spots are. Wind is likely to be funnelled through corridors between buildings, for instance. Although it is a bad idea to site greenhouses close to large trees, smaller shrubs and hedges can act as a windbreak. Reducing the amount of wind will mean lower fuel bills.

KEY

This symbol denotes the shadiest parts of the garden, typically to be found wherever a tree or building casts a shadow.

The yellow line denotes sunshine in the garden. On one side the sun will shine in the morning, on the other, in the afternoon.

This blue arrow denotes the direction of wind. In this case, the wind swirls over the wall and across the border beneath.

This green arrow denotes a gradient in the garden floor. In this case, the garden slopes from one end to another.

wind is strongest here

too cold to site here if greenhouse was to be a cool or warm house

cold spots will be worse if you site the greenhouse down the gradient

don't site too close – leaves and branches will fall off and may cause breakages

fence offers protection from wind and the cold

sunny a.m. and shady p.m.

sunny late a.m. until evening

Orientation It is generally thought best to place a greenhouse with its ridge along an east to west axis. This is so that one of its long, glazed sides is south facing, thus capturing the maximum amount of sun possible. Lean-tos should ideally be placed against a west-facing wall. This provides sunlight in the afternoon and evening to warm up the wall, which then releases heat through the night. East-facing walls are also suitable, although the greenhouse will then only get sun in the morning. A south-facing lean-to is too warm in summer for most plants, and will have to be used for real sun lovers only. A north-facing lean-to can only be used for real shade lovers.

Proximity Finally, it is a good idea to site your greenhouse as close as possible to the house. Proximity to the house can make it easier to connect up to mains electricity and water. If you are not intending to have the greenhouse connected up, siting it close to the house will make it easier to carry fuel and watering cans to it.

Making the foundations

Foundations for conservatories should ideally be made by professionals, as it is important to avoid problems with drainage, damp proofing and access to inspection chambers. Greenhouses can be erected directly onto firm ground, but it is a good idea to create a proper foundation if possible. Some greenhouse manufacturers recommend and supply bases, and these are the best to use in such cases. Small greenhouses are often fixed in place with

the use of ground anchors. To secure them, dig out a hole to the depth of the ground anchor and loosely fill it with rubble before inserting the ground anchor. Once it is in place, pour a concrete mix in and allow to set.

If you are laying foundations you will need to decide how you want the floor to be laid out before you start. Many people opt for a path down the middle with a border either side, but you can have a concrete floor and grow everything in containers or grow bags. If you want a completely concrete floor, mark out an area just larger than the greenhouse base, dig out the whole area to a depth of 100–125mm (4–5in) and fill with equal layers of hardcore, for the sub-base, and a concrete mix fluid enough to find its own level. If you are going to have an earth floor with a path, dig out a trench just large enough for the walls of the greenhouse to sit on comfortably. Fill this with hardcore and secure the ground anchors in place, then follow with the fluid concrete mix. A 100mm (4in) layer of hardcore and 100mm (4in) layer of concrete will be sufficient. Keep any topsoil removed from the trenches to use in borders inside your greenhouse.

Connecting to mains services

Although it is possible to heat, water and light a glasshouse without mains services, life is much easier with access to water and electricity. It is far easier to put these services in when planning a greenhouse than it will be at a later stage, so consider early on whether

Although foundations are not necessary, they will provide a basis for a more solid-standing structure when any greenhouse is erected

a concrete trench should be just large enough for the walls of the greenhouse to fit on comfortably

plants can be grown directly into the ground if desired

a hardcore sub-base provides the concrete with the best foundation on which to sit you will find them useful. Electric lighting can be used for working in the evenings and also for boosting plant growth in winter months, as well as encouraging some plants to flower out of season. Electric heaters are easy to use and have no fumes, but they can be expensive to run. Most small propagators use electricity. If you are not connecting the greenhouse up to the water mains, think about how far you will have to carry water and that this could become a major job during the hot summer months.

Only when everything is in place should you tighten screws

TIP

If you want an electric or gas supply to heat the greenhouse or a permanent supply of water, then employ a qualified electrician or plumber. Do not rely on an odd job man, a landscape gardener or a greenhouse erector to do these jobs.

Assembly

If you are including a brick base wall in your design, it is a good idea to employ a qualified builder, as bricklaying is a skilled job. Make sure that they follow the manufacturer's instructions carefully. People without specialist skills can carry out all other parts of constructing a greenhouse, although you may find it simpler to employ someone to do the whole job. The manufacturer should provide detailed instructions on putting together your particular greenhouse, but there are a few general points that are worth bearing in mind when assembling it.

• First, check that all parts have been supplied – there is nothing worse than getting half way through the job before realising a vital part is missing.

• When unpacking the parts, try to return them immediately to their correct boxes, to avoid confusion later on.

• When putting the frame together, make sure you do it in the correct order, and use a plumb line and spirit level as you go.

Use a spirit level at all times during construction

• Tighten screws only lightly at first, until the whole framework is in place. Once every part is in place and everything is level, you can tighten screws properly.

• Glazing will take place in a particular order and you should follow the manufacturer's instructions on this.

• Once glazing is completed, test for water tightness by spraying the whole structure with a hose. Make a note of the locations of any leaks and fill them with silicone sealant once the greenhouse is dry.

FLOORING FOR A CONSERVATORY OR GREENHOUSE

Conservatory flooring In a conservatory you will have a large choice of attractive floor coverings to choose from. There is such a wide variety of styles, colours and textures to choose from that even if you have paid for a particular company to build your conservatory, you can buy flooring elsewhere if their range does not suit. It is worth remembering that you will need to damp down the floor from time to time to raise humidity, so choose a floor covering that will not be affected by this.

Greenhouse flooring Most people opt to hard landscape at least the centre of the greenhouse, to provide a path to walk on. While you could leave the ground as soil, it will get extremely muddy in wet weather and you will have problems with weeds. A series of paving stones laid down the centre of the floor of the house will suffice, although the path will be safer and longer lasting if you fix the paving slabs in place.

Follow these steps for laying paving slabs:

• Dig out the path to the depth of the paving slabs, plus an extra 85mm (3⅜in).

• Fill the base of this trench with around 50mm (2in) of hardcore followed by 35mm (1⅜in) of sharp sand.

• Level the whole area out well using a rake and then tamp down to compact the sand and hardcore.

• Lay all of the slabs in place to get their positions correct.

• Mix a mortar of one part cement to four parts sand.

• Lift each slab in turn and place fist-sized amounts of mortar on the sand – one for each corner and one for the centre of the slab.

• Use a spirit level and a mallet to make sure each is level.

• Once the mortar has dried, brush a dry mortar mix of one part cement to three parts sand into the cracks in between the slabs and carefully water the area.

You could leave the areas both sides of the path as soil, but this is really only practical if you plan to grow plants directly in it. Do not use the greenhouse border soil to grow annual vegetables, as after a few years you will get problems with a build up of pests and diseases. Border soil should only be used to grow long-living perennial plants in, such as feature ornamental plants or fruit trees. Any other areas can be covered in a weed-suppressing membrane and then covered in gravel.

Conservatory flooring can be extremely decorative – it all depends on your own particular tastes

Planning Your Greenhouse or Conservatory

Once you have the basic framework of your greenhouse or conservatory in place, there are a few more things you will need to consider before putting in plants. Taking some time to plan the space and the way you are going to use it will help to make it easier to manage and lead to happier and healthier plants.

Staging brings plants up to eye level

Planning the space

It is, of course, possible to simply place pots and grow bags on the ground, but this does not make the most of the area, and you will find it hard to tend plants properly if they are not at a higher level.

Benches and staging These bring plants up to eye level and create more space. By using benches with slatted tops, some light will filter through to the lower levels and you will be able to grow plants that thrive in shade or dappled shade there. However, they are not so useful as propagation areas and are not suitable if you are using a capillary mat to aid watering.

   Try to keep one area free of benches for growing tall plants such as tomatoes. Alternatively, you can buy benches that fold away so that the way you use the space changes from season to season.

Propagation area Even if you only have a small area available, it is worth having some space for propagation. This should ideally include a solid bench, which provides a good surface for taking cuttings and which soil will not fall through. However, if you have a small space and have

Mobile potting trays are ideal for small spaces

opted for a slatted bench you can buy small mobile plastic or metal potting trays, which are surfaces with curved sides to keep compost in. They can be used for potting on smaller plants and for taking cuttings. Another feature of this area should be a heated propagator. This is a plastic box that is plugged into an electrical socket. It provides heat from below to help seeds to germinate and cuttings to root, and it has a clear plastic, tightly fitting lid that lets in light and holds in moisture. It is the perfect environment for cuttings and seedlings without the need to heat the whole greenhouse. Choose the largest propagator that is practical for your greenhouse, as it is bound to be in great demand each spring.

Shelves Shelves at eye level create useful extra space and are particularly good for displaying flowering plants. They will only be suitable for sun lovers, however, as there may be little shade available near the roof of the greenhouse.

Specimen plants When planning your space you need not know where you want every plant to be, but you do need to think about larger specimen plants and decide

Slatted benches allow light to filter through.

where to put them, and whether you are going to plant them directly into the soil. Some plants, most notably vines, benefit from having their feet in the soil outside of the greenhouse, to help ensure constant moisture at the roots, while the rest of the plant is grown inside. Growing vines in this way will require forward planning, as a pane of glass will have to be removed when the vine is planted.

Planning a conservatory In a conservatory you are unlikely to put in benches as permanent features: anything used to place plants on is likely to also function as furniture. However, it helps to plan the space. Increase the amount of space available to plants by using hanging

baskets, tiered plant holders and shelving. Think about your plants' needs and place closer to inside walls if they love shade or closer to glass walls if they are sun lovers. Larger, sun loving plants can shade smaller shade lovers.

Temperature
Choosing the right range

An essential part of setting up your greenhouse is deciding what temperature you would like to keep it at. This will affect the kinds of plants that you can grow.

Cold house An unheated greenhouse, known as a cold house, will always be warmer than the temperature outside and so will increase the range of plants to grow. However, the temperature will drop below freezing and so it is not suitable for anything that is frost tender. Cold houses are good for extending the growing season of vegetables, and for providing a more protected environment for tomatoes, peppers, cucumbers and vines. Cacti, succulents and alpines will all grow well in them, as they need protection from winter wet more than from the cold. Bulbs grown in pots will flower three to four weeks earlier than they would outdoors. A cold greenhouse is also a good place to grow hardy plants with early flowers that need some protection, most notably camellias.

Cool house The benefit of a greenhouse is really felt when a little heating is given in the winter months to keep it frost-free. A greenhouse kept at a minimum temperature of 4.5–7°C (40–45°F) is known as a cool house. A cool house greatly increases the range of plants that can be grown and gives you a place to overwinter non-hardy plants that spend summer in the garden. They are good places to start off early crops, to raise bedding plants for outside and to grow houseplants. This is the most popular type of greenhouse, as it is relatively cheap to heat and provides good conditions for a wide range of plants.

Warm house A warm greenhouse requires a minimum temperature of around 10–13°C (50–55°F). This means providing heating for a large part of the year, leading to high fuel bills. Many subtropical plants can be grown in these conditions.

Hot house A hot house has a minimum temperature of 15.5–18°C (60–64°F), great for growing tropical plants. It needs heat all year round, which makes fuel costs high.

Heating

It is a good idea to invest in a thermometer that shows minimum and maximum temperatures reached. The old-fashioned version has small iron temperature indicators

A minimum–maximum thermometer is ideal for a greenhouse

that stick at the highest and lowest temperature points. They can be reset with a magnet. There are also digital versions available.

These thermometers give you a good idea of how effective your heating system is. However, it is also possible to buy heaters with thermostats that will monitor the temperature of the air and switch on and off as necessary. This allows for peace of mind and prevents fuel being used when it is not needed.

Electric heaters The most popular type of heater for greenhouses is an electric fan heater, as this circulates air effectively. They are fairly small, easy to use and give off no fumes. Another popular choice is an electric tube heater. This is positioned a few inches away from the greenhouse wall and tucked away under the benches. It is good for providing the higher levels of heat needed in a warm or hot house. Electric heating cables are run over the benches and the plants are placed on top of them. They will prevent plants being harmed by the worst of cold weather. If you are using them in a cool greenhouse, remember that you will need some other form of heating to heat the air around the plants.

Electric fan heaters are the simplest form of greenhouse heating

Tube heating is a popular heating method in warm or hot houses

TIP

Place sensing devices at plant level in the greenhouse. Thermostats hung at eye level are easy to read but can provide incorrect values. Do not place thermostats in the direct rays of the sun, as this will obviously result in poor readings.

Gas heaters The simplest gas heaters to use are those that work from natural gas, but a supply will need to be installed by a qualified gas fitter. Heaters that run off bottled gas are also available, with the added benefit of producing carbon dioxide, which promotes plant growth. However, they also emit water vapour and the added moisture in the atmosphere can lead to an increase in plant disease problems. Conservatories may be heated by extending the central heating system. Once installed, this is a simple and effective method of heating.

Paraffin heaters While electricity and gas are the most straightforward fuels to use, they are also the most expensive. Paraffin heaters are cheaper to run, but they produce fumes and water vapour, and are hard to control.

Whichever type of fuel you decide on, get the right size heater for your greenhouse. Consult the manufacturer about the correct size for your house, taking into consideration the temperature you would like to keep it at.

Insulation

If you are going to heat your greenhouse or conservatory in winter, it is essential to insulate it. Even the most basic insulation will cut down fuel bills dramatically. Most conservatories can be supplied with double-glazing. While this is far more expensive to install than single

glazing, fuel bills for heating the area will be greatly reduced. In a greenhouse you will usually need to provide your own insulation for the winter months. This involves tacking or stapling a layer of transparent plastic to the framework of your greenhouse, creating a gap of about 25mm (1in) between the glass and the plastic, mimicking double-glazing. Bubble wrap is a good insulating material and can be tacked on closer to the glass, as it has its own insulating bubbles of air trapped within it.

Be aware that insulating the greenhouse in any way other than double-glazing cuts down the amount of light that the plants inside the house will receive. This can have a serious impact in winter, when light is already low.

> **TIP**
> Before winter sets in, check over the greenhouse for cracks and broken panes of glass, as heat will be lost through leakage. If there are no plants growing in the ground cover the soil with paving, gravel or sheeting to insulate the floor.

Ventilation

As well as heating the greenhouse and conservatory, it is important to consider cooling it down in warm weather. Even in cold weather, the greenhouse will need a regular change of air to prevent the atmosphere becoming stuffy.

A lack of fresh air provides the perfect environment for diseases. In warm weather, a change of air can be a lifesaver for overheated plants. To avoid overheating, your greenhouse should be equipped with plenty of ventilators. There should be ventilators in both the roof and the walls, so air can circulate freely. Attachments can be fitted to vents that push them open when the temperature rises and pull them closed when it falls. These are helpful if you are not able to constantly monitor your greenhouse. Consider fitting an extractor fan into the wall of the greenhouse or having a freestanding fan within the greenhouse to help the air to circulate.

Light
Providing shade

Generally, the idea is to get as much light as possible into your greenhouse to encourage high rates of growth. However, even plants can have too much of a good thing. At the height of summer the high levels of light and heat from the sun can become destructive. Plants can overheat and wilt, and leaves can be scorched. It can also become an uncomfortable place to work during the summer.

Shading paint The simplest way to provide shade for plants is to paint a shading paint over the outside of the whole structure when the weather starts to heat up around late spring and early summer. This paint is cheap and can be easily washed off before winter. However, it is not very flexible. In a dull summer, for instance, there will be many days when shading is not needed. It is impractical to regularly wash off and reapply shading paint.

Blinds Blinds are a more flexible, if more expensive, shading system. They are usually made out of wood or plastic and hung on the outside of the greenhouse. They can be rolled up or down depending on the brightness and the heat of the day. There are also blinds available that are hung on the inside of the greenhouse. This makes it easier to open and close windows and vents – outside blinds can restrict the amount that they can open, cutting down on ventilation. However, hanging blinds inside the greenhouse means that the light is only deflected away from the plants once it is already inside the structure. This means that greenhouses with indoor blinds heat up far more quickly than those with blinds on the outside, making them much less effective.

Automatic blinds It is possible to buy automatic blinds that will roll down when the sun is out and roll up again when the weather is cloudy. These automated systems respond to the temperature within the greenhouse. They

TIP

It is important to remove shading, whether provided by paints or blinds, in autumn. In winter your plants will need as much sunlight as they can get, so give painted greenhouses a good wash down and remove blinds.

are expensive, but will ensure your plants have the best conditions, even if you are not around to move blinds up and down according to changing weather. They are particularly useful for people who work full time and who are not able to monitor their greenhouses during the day.

Providing artificial lighting

Just as there are times when your greenhouse will need extra shade, so there are times it may need extra light. There are two reasons for this. The first is to improve the conditions for working after the sun has gone down. A bulb or lamp will increase the amount of time you can spend in the greenhouse after dark. This is not usually necessary in summer, as the length of the days mean that only the most devoted of greenhouse gardeners will need to go on working after night has fallen. However, in early spring, when there is seed sowing and other jobs to be done, a little extra light to work by can make a big difference. If you have electricity in your greenhouse, it is easy to plug in an electric light to work by.

The second reason for providing artificial lighting is to improve your plants' performance. You can encourage them to keep growing in winter by increasing light levels, but the most usual use of lighting is to encourage flowering, often out of season. Some plants need specific day lengths to flower and this can be provided in a

Applying shading paint to the outside provides protection for plants in the summer

Blinds are a more flexible way of providing shade

greenhouse if you have a timer system. Others simply benefit from a little extra light in the run up to flowering. If you are planning to try this, it is important to read up on your plants beforehand. Not all plants appreciate extra light: in fact, it can sometimes inhibit flowering if given at the wrong time.

Normal electric light bulbs are not much use as supplementary lighting. You will have to buy daylight bulbs or Gro-Lux tube lights to ensure that the light the plants are receiving is of the right wavelength.

Water

When setting up your greenhouse it is worth considering how easy it will be to water your plants. If you have mains water run up to the greenhouse, this will make your life easier than if you have to carry water from another point. A tap inside the greenhouse will allow you to easily fill up a watering can or to use a lance on the end of a hosepipe. This is perhaps the most straightforward way of watering. It is also the most time consuming but the most effective, as you can vary the amount of water given to each plant in a way you cannot do with automatic watering systems.

Capillary matting The simplest automatic watering system uses capillary matting laid across greenhouse benches. The matting is kept moist by being dipped into a reservoir of water at one end or simply watered with a watering can. Plants in plastic pots are placed onto the moist matting. The plants' compost is in direct contact with the moist matting and so moisture is drawn up into the pot and taken up by the roots.

> **TIP**
>
> There is no set rule for watering plants – it can even be viewed as an art. Touch the surface of the soil or other medium. If it is only slightly moist, it probably needs water. Observe the plants – if they become slightly wilted, water well.

Overhead sprinklers help create a humid atmosphere

Overhead watering A more sophisticated, but not necessarily better, form of automatic watering uses overhead sprinklers to water all plants for a set amount of time. They can be turned on and off manually or set to switch themselves on and off. The benefits are that plants are watered well, on a regular basis, and so are unlikely to suffer from periods of drought. This is a particular advantage to crop plants such as tomatoes, which benefit from having a constantly moist soil. Overhead watering also creates a humid atmosphere and eliminates the need for damping down. However, some plants do not thrive in these conditions, and it can be hard to keep drought-loving plants, such as cacti and succulents, dry enough under an automatic watering system.

Trickle irrigation Trickle irrigation is another form of automatic watering that uses pipes to get the water to the plants. Small pipes, connected to a larger pipe, are stuck into the surface of each pot. Water is fed along the larger pipe and trickles out into the containers. This system is useful in that everything is well watered, but with the same drawbacks as overhead irrigation: everything receives the same amount of water.

Caring for the Plants

Buying plants

Once you have decided what plants you want, you will need to find a good retailer. For more tropical plants, many garden centres have large, purpose-built indoor plant areas with plenty of light and a constant temperature, where trained staff maintain the plants and are on hand to offer advice. Don't forget to also look at outside displays in summer – many plants that are suitable for conservatories will be found out of doors in warmer weather. You may be lucky enough to have a specialist conservatory plant nursery nearby. If so, these are definitely the best places to buy from. You can see where the plants have been grown and can talk directly to the grower about the best plants to choose for the environment in your conservatory or greenhouse.

Some supermarkets have occasional deals on plants. However, supermarket conditions are far from perfect. Plants are likely to have been kept away from natural light, sometimes in draughty conditions and looked after by untrained staff, so they are best avoided, even if the price is tempting.

Buying strong, healthy plants is the best way of creating an impressive display in your greenhouse. Plants that are bursting with health will be far more likely to have a long and healthy life than those that are struggling from the start.

Checking the plant over Remember a few golden rules to make sure you get the best of the bunch when choosing plants. If you have a choice of a few plants, check where the plant emerges from the compost and choose the one with the most stems. These plants will be bushier and have a better eventual shape than those with single stems.

Look at the tips of the plant for new growth, which should be lighter green and more pliable than the older growth. Some new growth is a good sign, but lots of floppy new foliage can be a sign that the plant has been forced with too much heat and light. This can lead to the plant collapsing if it doesn't receive identical amounts of heat and light in your conservatory or greenhouse. Do not buy anything with dead or browning foliage. Marked down plants on bargain shelves with just a little damage are tempting, but try to resist the urge to nurse plants back to health. There is usually a reason for their decline and they will only get worse. Weeds on the surface of the compost suggest neglect and are a sign that the plant has not been potted up for a long time.

Inspecting the rootballs If you have a chance, carefully tip the plant out of its pot and inspect the roots. They should be white and look as if they have only recently reached the sides of the pot. A mass of roots implies that the plant has been in the same pot for too long. When potted into a larger pot or into the greenhouse border these roots will stay in a tight clump and continue circling the rootball, rather than growing out into the new compost.

Conversely, lots of loose compost surrounding a small rootball is a sign that

TIP

When buying bamboos, plants in very small pots are likely to be recently taken cuttings and may not have matured. These will take a lot more nurturing than more established specimens. Look for a plant in an 18cm (7in) pot or larger.

Avoid plants with browning foliage

Weeds suggest neglect

Buying bargain plants may be counter-productive

Scentsational Houseplants!

A healthy rootball is a good sign

Experienced garden centre staff will put your plant in a plastic sleeve or bag

make sure the plant is wrapped in a plastic sleeve or bag, or in paper. Experienced plant retailers should do this automatically. There is not such a need for this if plants have been bought from outdoor displays.

In summer, plants can get overheated and wilt if they are placed in a hot car or car boot. Make sure there is lots of ventilation to keep the plant cool on the journey home. Ensure the plant is well secured, as damage can be caused by the plant rolling around in the car.

Where to position Once you have got the plant home, you will need to decide where to position it within the greenhouse or conservatory. The most important factor to consider is how much light the plant needs. If it is a sun lover, it should be positioned on the benches or even the shelves of your greenhouse, or in an open position in the conservatory. If it is a shade lover, it can be placed underneath benches in the greenhouse. In a conservatory, position shade lovers underneath larger plants that cast a shadow. You can group large plants together to create a pool of shade for a few plants.

Soil requirements

Some plants will be planted directly into a conservatory or greenhouse border, but the majority are likely to need be planted into their own pots. Each plant has its own requirements and planting them into individual pots allows you to control the sort of soil they are in and the amount of water they receive.

the plant has been put into a larger pot just before being put on sale. Some nurseries do this so that they can charge more for the plant than they would be able to in a small pot. It is generally not a good sign and these plants should be avoided.

If you are buying a flowering plant, do not go for the one with the most flowers, but instead look for one that still has lots of unopened buds. The open flowers on the plant will quickly fade but buds suggest that the best show is still to come.

Getting them home If you buy a conservatory plant from an indoor display, it can get a shock from the change in temperature when you first take it outdoors to transport it home. Wind and direct sunlight can also take their toll on delicate foliage. To avoid these problems,

Secure your plants well to prevent damage

Orchids thrive best in a coarse mix of grit, peat and bark

24

General compost When choosing compost for most plants, go for good-quality, general-purpose compost. These are usually loam-based and are far easier to work with than peat-based composts, which are tricky to re-wet once they have dried out and do not hold nutrients well.

Specialist compost Some greenhouse and conservatory plants have particular needs and will benefit from specialist compost. In the wild, many orchids grow in open situations such as over rocks or on the branches of trees. Growing them in fine-textured compost, such as houseplant compost, will make the roots rot. Instead, they need a coarse mix of chopped bark, grit and peat, which will drain extremely freely. Cacti and succulents also need freely draining compost, but they can cope with one with a closer texture. A good mix is one-quarter grit or sand to three quarters houseplant compost. Azaleas and cyclamen are among a group of plants known as lime haters that need a slightly acid soil in order to thrive. The best soil for them is called ericaceous compost. Compost mixes for orchids, cacti and succulents and lime haters are available from garden centres.

Potting on

Any plants that are kept in pots for the whole of their lives benefit from some fresh compost occasionally. To avoid checking growth, most should be potted on into a slightly larger pot each year. This gives them some fresh compost to grow into, preventing the roots from getting

Put pieces of broken pot over drainage holes

congested. Pot plants on at the beginning of spring when the plants are just starting into growth.

To pot on, carefully tip the plant out of its existing pot. If it does not come out easily, hold the pot upside-down and tap the edge of the pot against the edge of a bench or table. You can also push the plant out through the drainage holes.

If roots are congested, tease them out carefully. This will encourage them to grow into the new compost, rather than circling the existing rootball. Pull away some of the compost from the surface of the rootball. If using a terracotta pot, place some pieces of broken pot over the drainage hole to help drainage. Do not cover drainage holes if you are using a capillary mat for watering, as the soil in the pots needs to be in direct contact with the mat.

Fill the bottom 2.5cm (1in) or so of the pot with compost and place the plant onto it. Carefully feed compost down the sides of the rootball. Use your fingers to make sure there are no pockets of air and to firm down the compost. Then add more compost to the surface until it reaches the level of the old compost. Make sure the soil level is at least 2.5cm (1in) below the rim of the pot. This makes watering easier. Finally, water the plant in. You will not need to feed the plant for about a month.

Tease roots carefully to encourage growth into new compost

TIP

Another method of repotting into a larger container is to put the smaller pot into the larger one and fill round it with compost. Then remove the smaller pot, tap the plant out and drop it snugly into its new home.

Firm the newly potted plant into its new home

Check that decorative pots have drainage holes in the bottom

It is important not to re-pot into containers that are too large, or the plant will get waterlogged. To judge the right size, tip the plant out of its existing pot and lower the rootball into the new pot. There should be about 2.5cm (1in) of space at the bottom of the pot and your finger should easily fit between the rootball and the edge of the pot.

Top-dressing Not all plants need regular potting on. Some resent the root disturbance that comes with complete re-potting. Others perform best when their roots are confined and some are simply too large to be easily re-potted. These will all benefit from top-dressing (top-dressing is simply adding a layer of compost on the surface of a pot). Scrape off the top 2.5–4cm (1–1½in) of soil and replace with fresh compost. Water the fresh compost in.

Choosing containers

There is a great range of pots available from garden centres that are suitable for indoor plants. The main choice you will need to make is between terracotta and plastic. Each has its benefits and drawbacks. Plastic pots are cheap and easy to get hold of, they are light and easy to move, contain moisture well, and will not break if dropped. They are also the best pots to use if you are watering the plants via a capillary mat. However, many people prefer the natural appearance of terracotta and their added weight can be helpful with large, top-heavy plants. Glass fibre pots can be moulded and coloured to look like stone, but are much lighter. Reconstituted

TIP

When buying a container, always check that there are adequate drainage holes. There are lots of decorative pots available without any. These pots are only useful as an ornamental container for another pot with drainage holes.

stone containers are crushed stone moulded into urns and vases, but are extremely heavy. Whichever type you choose, it is important to keep the same type throughout the life of the plant. Each creates quite different environments for the plant roots and growth may be checked if you change from one to the other.

Watering

How often you water the plants in your conservatory or greenhouse depends on many factors. First, you need to know the plants' particular needs. As a general rule, the thinner the leaf, the more water it needs. Succulents with their thick, fleshy leaves need less water than ferns with their paper-thin leaves.

The amount of water needed will also depend on the weather and the season. During hot spells in summer you may have to water many of the plants every day. As growth slows in winter it is essential to give plants less water. Too much water in autumn and winter will lead to plants sitting in water, which can make the roots rot. Plants in larger pots will need watering less often than those in small pots. The larger the volume of compost, the larger the amount of water that is held and the less likely the compost is to dry out. Therefore, tomatoes that are grown in grow bags will have a more even supply of water than those grown in all but the largest pots.

To find out when your plants need watering you must get to know them. Lift up and get used to the weight of the containers when they are dry and when watered. This way you will be able to assess when plants are drying out. You can also check the level of moisture in the compost by putting your fingers just under the surface of the compost. With a combination of these two methods, you should be able to tell when your plant needs watering.

Automatic watering If you install an automatic watering system you will have little choice in the way your plants are watered. They are either watered from below if using a capillary mat, from above if using an overhead sprayer or directly into the pot if you are using a trickle irrigation system. Of all of these systems the capillary mat is probably the most effective as it allows the plants to take up moisture as they need it. Overhead sprayers can cause problems because they wet the foliage. This can lead to scorched foliage in summer or can encourage moulds to develop in winter.

Manual watering If you are watering by hand, most plants can be watered from above using a houseplant watering can. They have long spouts that allow you to get past the leaves to water at the base of the plant, avoiding wetting the leaves. Some plants should be

Get used to the weight of a pot before and after watering

watered from below. These are usually plants such as Saintpaulia, which have fleshy, hairy leaves that might rot if water is left sitting on them. Fill the plant's drip tray with water and then leave the plant to take up the water. After half an hour check to see if all the water has been absorbed. If it has, you may want to try filling the tray again. If there is water left in the tray after a further hour, empty it.

Feel the compost to check how moist it is

GOING ON HOLIDAY

A well-stocked greenhouse is a big commitment, and you may find it hard to take a long summer holiday if you have one. It is only really an option if some of your greenhouse functions, such as watering and ventilation, are automated and you have a horticulturally minded neighbour or friend. Ask them to pop in and either water plants every couple of days or to check that the automated systems are working effectively. You could also group plants together so that they cast shade over each other, so minimising the amount of water they need to take up.

A long-spouted watering can avoids wetting the leaves

Humidity

High humidity is essential to keep greenhouse and conservatory plants healthy. Dry air can lead to leaves looking dried out and brown patches or edges appearing. Low humidity will also encourage one of the most common pests of greenhouse and conservatory plants – red spider mite. Most plants will reward any efforts to increase the humidity in the air around them by growing faster and having healthier foliage. Higher humidity reduces the amount of water that plants lose through their leaves. This in turn reduces their need for watering. Orchids and ferns in particular need high levels of humidity to grow well.

Ways to increase humidity There are several ways of increasing the humidity around plants. One of the simplest is to group plants together. Groups of plants will trap humidity within the canopy formed by their leaves. Regular misting with a fine spray is a good way of increasing humidity temporarily, but it will not improve humidity throughout the greenhouse or conservatory. Plants can be grown in a tray of expanded clay granules. These granules absorb water and release it slowly, so that the humidity around the plants remains

fairly constant. However, the most common and effective method of increasing humidity is damping down. This is quick and easy, and is suitable for all greenhouses and conservatories that have waterproof flooring. Damping down simply means watering the floor or benches. This is particularly effective on benches covered in capillary matting, as this absorbs the water well. The water then evaporates and increases the humidity evenly throughout the area, while reducing the temperature. From spring to autumn damp down at least once a day. In hot weather you will need to damp down several times a day.

Group orchids and ferns together to keep the humidity high

Cacti and succulents need little or no feeding during the winter months.

Food

Plants that are grown in greenhouse borders and those that are grown with their roots planted outside of the greenhouse will only need occasional feeding once they are established, as they have a relatively large area of soil to exploit for nutrients. It is those plants that will spend their whole lives in pots that need consideration. Such a small area of soil contains limited nutrients that are quickly used up. These plants will need regular feeding in order to remain healthy and look their best.

When to feed

Most composts contain enough fertilizer to feed a plant for a few months, so after first potting up a plant, or after potting on or top-dressing, you will not need to feed for a while. After a few months these nutrients will be depleted and this is the time to start feeding again. Some edible plants are in the ground for a short time and need feeding from early on to help them produce the maximum amount during their short life spans. Start feeding edibles such as tomatoes, peppers and cucumbers when the first fruits have set.

Most ornamental greenhouse and conservatory plants do not need feeding all year round. Plants in cold or cool greenhouses will benefit most if you start feeding at the same time as watering is increased in spring. Feed regularly throughout summer and decrease towards autumn as growth slows. Stop feeding altogether when the plants go into their winter resting phase. In warm or hot houses, plants may keep growing for a much longer period of the year, and you may need to keep feeding longer and start feeding earlier in spring than you would for other plants. However, all plants should be given a resting period when their feed and watering is reduced for a while.

Choosing fertilizers

The most important distinction to make when choosing a fertilizer is between those designed for flowering plants and those for foliage plants. All fertilizers contain nitrogen, phosphate and potash. Nitrogen is responsible for strong, leafy growth, phosphate keeps roots healthy and potash encourages flowering. For leafy plants choose a fertilizer with a good balance of these three or with a higher percentage of nitrogen. For flowering and fruiting plants choose a fertilizer with extra potash. For some plants, such as tomatoes, you

Fruiting plants, such as *Capsicum annuum* 'Hungarian Hot Wax', will need a feed with extra potash

Slow-release fertilizer pellets are added to compost

TIP

Whenever you use slow-release granules or feed sticks in your containers, remember to keep a note of when you added them or put them in, so that you know when they have finished being effective.

Food blocks release nutrients gradually

will be able to purchase a fertilizer that has been designed specifically for their needs. Tomato fertilizers contain high levels of potash to encourage flowers to form and to aid the development of fruit.

Liquid feed Using liquid fertilizer is among the best ways of feeding plants in pots, as it allows complete control over the timing and amount of feed. A small amount of liquid fertilizer is added to a set amount of water and is watered into the plant. Most ornamental plants will need feeding once every few weeks, but check their individual requirements.

Slow-release pellets Slow-release fertilizer pellets can be useful. They are simply added to the soil at re-potting stage or sprinkled on the surface of the compost in spring and will feed the plant all season. They are less versatile

than liquid feeds, as the strength of the feed cannot be altered. If the pellets are added late in the season there is a danger that the feed could continue into autumn and winter, when feeding should have stopped.

Feed sticks Feed sticks are another way of cutting down on the chore of feeding. These are small sticks or blocks of concentrated feed that are pushed into the soil and gradually release nutrients. They have similar draw-backs to slow-release fertilizers in that there is less control over timing and concentration of feeds than with liquids. They also concentrate feed in one area of the pot, which may lead to uneven growth.

If using a liquid fertilizer, feed most plants once every two weeks during the growing season. Check the individual requirements of your plant to find out if it needs more or less frequent application of feed, or if it needs the feed to be more dilute than that used for most plants. This is often the case for orchids, but can apply to other plants too.

Regular feeding has resulted in a greenhouse full of healthy plants

down and dunked into a bowl of tepid water. Some leaves will also benefit from a polish with leaf shine or plant wipes, which can be bought from garden centres. Plant leaves dull as they age and leaf shine restores their natural glossiness. It is only necessary to use polish on older leaves as young leaves have a natural shine. Plants with hairy or non-shiny leaves may not look like they need cleaning as much as those with shiny leaves, but they also need dust removed occasionally to allow them to get enough light. Buy a small, soft brush and use it to carefully clean off dust and dirt from the surface of the leaves and from the stems.

Cleaning

Cleaning plants

By erecting a greenhouse you are making a huge effort to give your plants high light levels in order to make them grow quicker. However, by simply failing to clean the plants themselves, you are dramatically reducing the amount of light that reaches them. Cleaning is often overlooked, but it can make a big difference to the health and appearance of your plants. As well as stopping light and air from reaching the leaves, and so slowing growth, dust and limescale deposits from misting make plants look neglected.

The plants that need cleaning most often are the foliage plants. Many of these have glossy leaves that show up dust. Wash the leaves carefully with a sponge and then wipe dry with a soft cloth. Small plants can be turned upside

> **TIP**
>
> If you want to clean the leaves in one go with a gentle shower, place aluminum foil over the top of the pot to prevent the soil from splashing out while you wash the plant all over.

Cleaning the greenhouse

Just as dirt on the leaves will reduce the amount of light that reaches the plants, so will dirt on the glass. There is little point in going through the effort of erecting a greenhouse if you are not going to keep the glass clean. In fact, it is a good idea to clean the whole structure once a year and then to occasionally clean the glass throughout the year. Over time dirt builds up in cracks, crevices and corners, and small bits of rubbish get left under benches. It is in these sheltered and neglected spots that pests and diseases often make winter homes for themselves from which they sally forth and attack your plants the following spring.

When to clean The best time to have a good clean up of your greenhouse or conservatory is in the autumn. Because this is after the cropping of most edible plants has already taken place, it minimises disruption in the greenhouse. Choose a mild day when your plants will not be too affected by low temperatures. Move everything

Wash all panes – inside and out – with warm, soapy water or disinfectant

TIP

Tidy up any plant debris, weeds, dead leaves and flowers, remove sick and dying plants, and sweep up regularly throughout the year. This helps reduce fungal disease, and removes any debris and weeds that would harbour pests.

disinfectant and start at the ridge of the greenhouse, cleaning all panes and supports well. Make sure you open all vents and windows and wash them thoroughly. As you work your way through the greenhouse, pay particular attention to corners or awkward nooks and crannies. These are the bits that are most likely to get neglected at other times of the year and therefore places where pests are most likely to hide out. Clean the path thoroughly with disinfectant. If you have access to a pressure sprayer use this to clean algae and other dirt from the path and to get into the awkward corners.

Once the whole house has been cleaned you will need to wash off the disinfectant. Start by hosing down the outside of the greenhouse and then move inside. Once everything is clean, leave it for a couple of hours to dry out before you move the plants back in.

During this time, you could take the opportunity to sort the plants out. Clean the outside of their containers, as these can often become splattered with dirt, and remove any dead growth. Throw out tomato, pepper and cucumber plants that have finished fruiting, cleaning off any bamboo canes or other supports. Wash out any loose pots or seed trays that you are going to put back into the greenhouse at the same time.

out of the greenhouse or indoors if the weather is cool or you have particularly tender plants. Once everything is out, clear away any rubbish and give the whole structure a brush over, including any benches and paths. Once this is done you can start cleaning.

Cleaning the outside Starting with the outside of the greenhouse, you will need a sturdy ladder and a mop. The long handle of the mop will help you to reach the whole of the roof. Wash off any shading paint, as well as any debris that has collected on the roof. This is also a good time to check over guttering to make sure that it has not become cracked or blocked. Use warm, soapy water (you can buy a suitable disinfectant from garden centres) to wash all of the panes of glass, all the time taking care to clean the supports between each pane of glass well.

Cleaning inside Indoors, the cleaning will need to be extremely thorough. Take a fresh bucket of warm water and

If the greenhouse has guttering, don't forget to clean it out

Training

One of the real treats of owning a greenhouse or conservatory is the range of beautiful ornamental climbers that you find yourself able to grow. In order to appreciate them best it is essential to provide them with lots of support. This helps them to grow into a good shape, prevents foliage from becoming too wayward and allows the plant to show off its blooms properly.

Supports for smaller climbers can consist of a wire frame in the shape of a hoop or circle, or a tripod of bamboo canes, pushed into the soil of the container they are growing in. Pieces of trellis small enough to push into the soil at the edge of the pot can also be used. However, for larger climbers, and to create really impressive displays, it makes sense to erect a more permanent support. Conservatories and lean-tos come into their own here, as there is usually a solid house wall available for plants to climb up. These are the places on which to attach supports for the larger climbers.

Erecting trellis A piece of solid wooden trellis can be attached to a wall, providing the perfect climbing frame for most climbers. Before erecting it, take two pieces of wood the same length as the height of the trellis and at least 5cm (2in) thick. Attach them to the wall using screws. If you are fixing screws into masonry, it's best to use a cordless drill with the correct size of masonry bit. Once you have drilled a hole, push a rawlplug into it to support the screw. The pieces of wood should be attached vertically and spaced so that the outer edges of the trellis can be screwed onto them. This will ensure that the trellis is far enough away from the wall to allow growth to twine freely around it, as well as for air to circulate.

Using wire The other system used for supporting large climbers is that of horizontal wires. Vine eyes are screwed into the wall and wires stretched horizontally between them. A series of horizontal wires approximately 30cm (12in) apart will provide ample support for a climber.

Other supports A number of plants use aerial roots that emerge from their stems as a method of climbing. You will need to provide a moss pole for these plants (a pole made from chicken wire filled with moss). Tomatoes, cucumbers, melons and vines need support as they grow. For tomatoes, a bamboo cane is usually adequate, as long as the growth is tied in regularly. Cucumbers, melons and vines really need more substantial support, so put up a set of horizontal wires. Trellis could be used but it is harder to remove the dead material from at the end of the season.

TIP Some non-climbing, standard plants may benefit from the light support of a single cane, pushed into the compost at the centre of the pot. This will help keep the plant straight and upright as it grows.

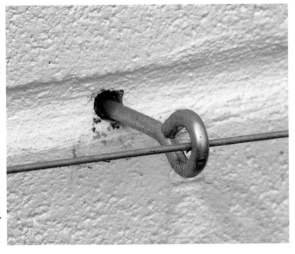

Vine eyes hold horizontal wires which support climbers

Screw trellis panels to free-standing posts or fix onto any solid part of the structure

33

How and when to train

If you are incorporating a support into the container it is always best to make sure the support is in place when first potting up the plant. This will help avoid damage that could be caused by forcing a support into the rootball of a plant. Although plants have their own climbing mechanisms, such as twining tendrils or stems, they need to be tied in to the frame to start them off and regular tying in as they grow, to encourage a good shape. Train plants in summer while the plant is still growing and growth is still flexible; it becomes woody and hard to manipulate in winter.

Some plants climb by producing aerial roots and these need a soft material to sink into. Moss poles are made out of chicken wire or similar material and filled with moss, and are perfect for these kinds of plants. Plants grown on moss poles should be loosely tied to the pole to encourage the aerial roots to take hold. Keep the pole moist at all times by misting or dribbling water onto it.

If you are providing a single cane to support a standard plant, take great care as you insert it, as it will need to be put into the centre of the root ball. Tie the main stem into the cane at regular intervals as the plant grows.

TIP

Many climbing plants bear more flowers on stems tied horizontally, or with growing tips pointing down, than they do on stems with growing points pointing up. Bear this in mind when you are training and you will be rewarded with more flowers or fruit – or both.

Fan-training a fruit tree

Apricots, peaches and figs are not climbers but can still be trained against a wall or side of a greenhouse. Training these plants into a fan shape or a series of tiers against a wall allows you to grow fruit without it taking over a lot of space. It does not harm the plants, in fact, it may help to promote extra flowering and fruiting. The movement of sap in apricots, peaches and figs is restricted by training, and so energy that would normally shoot up the stems and go into producing lots of lush, leafy growth is instead redirected into producing fruits. It is a good idea to set up a framework made of horizontal wires on which to train the fruit tree.

To prune a fruit tree into a fan you will need to start with a feathered maiden – a young tree with a few side branches. Cut back the new growth on the central stem to about half and select two strong side shoots on each side, pruning out all others. Space these out well and either tie them directly onto the wires or attach angled canes to the wires and tie them onto that. During the following season allow four strong side shoots to grow on each side and train them so that they fan out and fill any spaces. Remove all other shoots. This will provide you with the basic fan shape for your tree. Over subsequent years you will have to occasionally let a new shoot grow from the base to replace one of the older stems. Apart from that you should pinch out side shoots and nip out the tips of shoots to prevent the fan from becoming too large or overcrowded.

Training a fruit tree into a fan shape can be extremely useful if you are short of space in your conservatory or greenhouse

prune out all other shoots from the two main stems to leave four or five strong side shoots each

Routine pruning

Plants will always need a little pruning to keep them looking their best. With this in mind, there are a few simple pruning-type tasks you will need to carry out.

Deadheading Once a plant has flowered, its instinct is to try to set seed. If it is allowed to do this, it will put lots of energy into producing seed and little into producing more flowers. To prevent this happening, keep an eye on your flowering plants. As the flowers fade, gently nip them off the plant using your fingers. This will encourage the plant to produce more flowers. Conversely, with fruiting plants, you will not want to pinch out any of the flowers as you want to encourage as many fruits to form as possible.

Thinning out fruits However, once fruits have formed they may sometimes need thinning out. This is necessary most of all with vines. They often produce huge amounts of flowers and all of these will try to turn into fruits. However, vines are unable to bring large numbers of fruits to full maturity and so some will need to be removed early on. Wait until all of the flowers have set fruit – there is little point in removing flowers before this point as they may not all turn into fruit and you may end up removing the wrong ones. Using secateurs, snip off some of the small bunches of fruit so that there is only one bunch left for each 30cm (1ft) of stem. As the bunches swell, you will also need to thin out some of the grapes.

TIP Use hand pruners or a pair of sharp scissors to deadhead flowers that feature tougher, almost woody stems. Other flowers to snip include Aster, coneflower (Echinacea *spp*.), Coreopsis, Hosta, Zinnia, lilies and Rudbeckia.

Deadheading will help this azalea produce even more flowers

Nipping out All plants have strong hormones that encourage them to grow as large as possible. If a central stem is growing strongly, these hormones inhibit the growth of all the side shoots so that the lead shoot can grow quickly up to the light, often shedding lower leaves

Nipping the top of a plant will prevent it growing leggy

TIP

Drastic renovation is best carried out over at least two years. Leave some of the more upright shoots intact for better recovery. When the plant starts into growth again, it should be stronger and fuller than before.

as it goes. This natural instinct to grow as tall as possible can lead to plants becoming 'leggy' – tall, thin and straggly stalks, which have a difficult time supporting the weight of the plant. To prevent this, nip out the top pair of leaves with secateurs or with fingers and thumb. Once this strong growing point has been removed, the plant will spread its energy to the rest of the plant, making side shoots sprout and creating a bushy plant. You can repeat this many times over to keep the plant compact and bushy.

If parts of the plant have died back or become damaged they should be removed to prevent the problem spreading to other parts of the plant. Cut back into healthy growth.

Leaves of many plants such as ferns die back as a matter of course, so should be regularly removed to prevent build-up of dead material.

Pruning neglected plants

Sometimes plants need a bit of intensive care to get them actively growing and looking their best. This can happen if a plant has been neglected and left in the same pot for a number of years, or if it has not been regularly pruned and has lots of weak, leggy growth. Look towards the base of the plant and choose a point to cut back to. Choose the highest leaf that you would like to keep and then make a cut just above that leaf. Any stem left above that cut will die back, so cut pretty close, but be careful not to damage the leaf joint as this is where the next bud will emerge.

Carry out the same process across the whole plant. If the plant is really large, cutting it back hard can be a bit

of a shock and this can eventually kill the plant. If you are worried about doing this, carry out renovation pruning in two stages. Cut the plant back by about one third and then leave it for a few weeks until side shoots start to appear. Choose the lowest of the side shoots and cut back just above this.

If a plant has not been well cared for, there is a good chance that it will also need re-potting. Do this after your first prune. If the plant and pot are too large to re-pot, top dress with fresh compost. To lessen the shock of a severe prune, place the plant in a shady spot until it starts into growth. Then move it into bright, indirect light. Ensure the plant is kept well fed and watered.

When hard pruning, cut back to just above a leaf joint

Propagation

A greenhouse is perfect to increase your plant collection by propagation, as this place is completely under the gardener's control. It is shielded from the extremes of climate, meaning that the warm, moist atmosphere that most seedlings and cuttings require is fairly easy to create and maintain. It can be used to grow new plants for the greenhouse or home, to replace old and declining plants or as a gentle starting place for plants that will spend most of their lives out of doors.

Propagation is usually carried out in spring. This is because plants are actively growing, so cuttings are more likely to take than in a time of sluggish growth. Spring propagation also gives plants the maximum growing time to get established before growth slows in autumn. Bulbs are the exception. As many of them flower in spring, most need to be planted in autumn.

Sowing seeds

Many edible and ornamental plants that are grown in the greenhouse or conservatory can be easily propagated from seed. As a greenhouse is usually fairly warm and sheltered, many can simply be sown and left on benches, where they will soon germinate. However, when sowing in early spring, where temperatures can still drop, or if sowing plants that germinate slowly or erratically, it can be useful to use a propagator. This is a closed cabinet that is kept at a constant temperature. As it has a lid, humidity within it is fairly high. These conditions provide the perfect environment for germinating seedlings.

Step-by-step growing from seed

Take a seed tray or small pot and fill it with a fine compost, such as seed and cutting compost [A], before firming it down lightly. The size of the seed will affect how densely they should be sown. Fine seed should be sprinkled in a thin layer over the top of the compost [B],

Using a dibber, carefully hold the seedling by its leaves

TIP

You can pre-germinate seeds – make them sprout before sowing – by placing them between several layers of moist paper towel in a re-sealable plastic bag. Keep the bag warm, check seeds daily and plant those that have sprouted.

while large seeds may be sown one to a pot. Cover the seed with a light dusting of compost or with vermiculite. Water and place in your propagator or cover with a clear plastic bag to retain moisture.

Once seedlings have appeared and before they have grown too large to be disentangled from each other, they will need to be pricked out into individual pots so that they have the space to grow. Prepare the pots that the seedlings are going to be planted into first. They can be filled with the same fine seed and cutting compost mix as the seeds were sown into. Push the soil down gently to make sure there are no air pockets and then make a small

Water transplanted seedlings as soon as possible

indentation for the seedling to go into in the centre of the pot, using a specially designed dibber or a pencil. Turning to the tray or pot of seedlings, use the dibber to lift sections of the compost up before selecting a seedling with your fingers. Hold the seedling by the leaves – never by the delicate stem – as you gently work with the dibber to free it from the compost. The seedling should be placed into the pot and the soil pushed gently down around it to firm in its delicate roots. Water transplanted seedlings as soon as possible. If you have space, place these pricked out seedlings back into the propagator while they recover from the shock of transplantation.

Taking cuttings

When taking cuttings it is important to use a sharp knife or pair of secateurs. Clean cuts are less likely to get infected with rots than those that have been cut with blunt knives and have jagged edges. Keep tools clean and sharp. Most cuttings should be put into the soil straight away so that they do not lose any moisture. After taking cuttings, keep them in a sealed plastic bag and mist them with water to prevent them drying out.

The exception to this is succulents, which often contain too much water. This can lead to them rotting if they are put straight into the soil. To prevent this, leave cuttings to dry out for a couple of days before planting.

Leaf cuttings

There are several ways leaves can be used for propagation. One is to use the whole leaf, cut in certain places that are kept in contact with the soil. This is a particularly effective method for propagating begonias. Fill a small seed tray with seed and cutting compost.

Propagate begonias by whole leaf cutting

Select a healthy leaf and turn it face down before making a small cut across each of the main veins with a sharp knife. Place the leaf facing upwards onto the compost and pin down along the veins. Water and cover with a propagator lid or a clear plastic bag. Small plantlets will eventually appear along the veins. When they are large enough, tip the soil out of the tray and pot the plantlets up individually.

Part leaf cuttings are used to propagate Begonia and Streptocarpus. Fill a seed tray with compost. Slice a section of leaf about 4cm (1½in) in length and insert it into the compost. Keep watered until shoots appear. Pot each new plant into its own pot.

Stem cuttings

Cuttings taken from plant stems are the most common type of cutting and can be used to propagate a huge number of plants.

Softwood cuttings Softwood cuttings are so called because they are taken when growth is new and pliable.

Place cuttings in a clear plastic bag to keep them from drying out

A

B

They are usually the best type of cutting to use if you are propagating plants for the greenhouse, conservatory or home. These cuttings should be taken in spring after new growth has been put on but has only just started to harden up and ripen. When plant material is in this state, it has been actively growing and so is quicker to put down new roots. However, there are drawbacks with these cuttings. Because the growth has not hardened up, cuttings lose water quickly and may wilt before they have had a chance to put down roots. These cuttings, therefore, are only worth taking if you can provide an extremely protected environment, such as a propagator. In a propagator, high humidity is maintained, which prevents water being lost from the leaves, and bottom heat encourages the fast formation of roots.

To take softwood cuttings, use secateurs to remove a stem of new growth. Each cutting should be about 5cm (2in) in length. Prepare the bottom of the cutting by paring back to just below where a set of leaves emerge. Then, using a sharp knife, remove all but the top pair of leaves [A] and push the cutting into the compost [B]. Place several cuttings into the same pot. Roots should form within a few weeks and plants can then be potted on individually.

Semi-ripe cuttings Semi-ripe cuttings are taken later in the season, usually from mid- to late summer, when growth has started to harden up. This is a useful technique when using your greenhouse to propagate plants for the garden. Cuttings are tougher and will not wilt as easily as softwood cuttings, so they do not necessarily need to be grown in propagator. However, roots will take longer to form. The method is the same as for softwood cuttings.

TIP

Scrupulous cleanliness with tools is vital with propagation. Most processes involve cutting into plant tissue. All cuts must be made cleanly, either with a very sharp knife or with secateurs for thicker stems, and the tool cleaned after each cut.

Planting bulbs, tubers

Although plants that grow from bulbs and tubers can be bought in flower, it is extremely easy, and cheaper, to plant them yourself. Try to buy and plant them as soon as they become available. This will give them the longest possible time to grow and establish. Both bulbs and tubers can deteriorate in dry storage conditions, so the quicker you can get them into some compost, the better. The first thing to check when buying is how firm they feel. Any that are soft may have rotted. Do a visual check for dark or discoloured areas that could indicate rots. A complete skin, with no splits or tears in it, should cover bulbs.

Planting and caring for bulbs

Always plant bulbs into a pot with drainage holes and put some broken crocks in the bottom to ensure good drainage. As a general rule, bulbs should be planted at a depth two to three times their own length.

Plant bulbs at depth two or three times their length

Once they are planted, water well. Put in a cool, bright spot in the greenhouse and keep them watered throughout winter and early spring. In an unheated glasshouse, the flowers will appear a couple of weeks earlier than those planted outside, and even earlier in a heated greenhouse. Once flower buds have formed you can bring the plants into your house for flowering, although they will last longest and perform best in cool conditions, so simply enjoy them in the greenhouse.

After flowering, the pots of bulbs can be put outside. Keep watering and feeding after flowering and until the foliage dies down completely. This will feed the bulbs and ensure a good display of flowers the following year. Once

Keep bulbs in a cool place with each pot clearly labelled

following year. Throw them away or plant out in the garden. They will flower again a few years later.

Propagating from tubers

In winter, begonias die back to tubers. If they are kept fairly dry in their pots they will sprout again the following year. However, if you lift and divide them you can increase your stock. In winter, once the foliage has died down, remove the tubers from the pot and clean them off. Dust with fungicide and store in a dry place. In spring, place the tubers on the surface of a pot of well-drained compost until shoots appear. Then cut the tuber in half, ensuring that each section has a shoot. Pot each section up in its on pot.

the foliage has died down, remove the bulbs from the compost, cut off the dead foliage, clean the bulbs and leave in a cool, dry place until the following autumn.

Forcing bulbs

There are several ways of forcing bulbs so that they flower early. It is good fun trying to force bulbs so that they flower during winter and for this you will need to buy specially prepared bulbs from the garden centre. They are available at the same time as those for spring flowering, but should be treated differently. Plant the bulbs in a container and water in, and then place in a cool, completely dark spot outdoors for about ten weeks.

Keep the container moist during this time. Move the bulbs indoors about four weeks before you want them to flower, so for Christmas flowering this will mean early winter. Small shoots should have appeared. Place the container in a cool, bright place. Flower buds should appear after a few weeks. Continue watering throughout this time and turn the pot regularly to prevent all of the shoots growing towards the light.

After flowering, forced bulbs will be exhausted and will not flower the

TIP

Lay Dahlia tubers flat with the eye pointed up. Plant 8–15cm (3–6in) deep, 45–60cm (18–24in) apart. To avoid damaging the tubers, stake before or at planting. Do not water tubers when planting. Over watering early in the season can rot the tubers.

Cut canna tubers in half once shoots have appeared

Sowing plants for use in the garden

You should not think of only propagating to fill the greenhouse. Its potential usefulness for the rest of the garden is vast, so consider other plants that can be started off there. The most obvious group of plants are those that are not hardy, but need to be germinated before the danger of the last frost has passed. These plants fall into two main groups: tender or half-hardy bedding plants and early vegetable plants. All can be bought as seed, but gardeners without greenhouses are often forced to buy young plants at far higher prices, because they do not have the facilities to care for seedlings. These seeds should be sown the same as any others, although it is a good idea to grow them with some heat if possible. Start them off between late winter and early spring (check seed packets for exact timings) in a heated propagator and prick them out into individual pots as soon as they are large enough. They will need gradual hardening off to allow them to adjust to the difference in temperature between the greenhouse and the outdoors. The best place for this, if you have it, is a cold frame. Failing that, you can start off by putting plants outside during the day and bringing them in at night. You can also erect a temporary cloche over them when you first plant them out, to keep off the worst of the late winter or early spring cold and wet.

PLANTS TO BE STARTED OFF IN THE GREENHOUSE

Edible plants

Broad, French and runner beans	Lettuce
Cabbage	Pea
Cauliflower	Peppers
Celeriac	Pumpkin and squash
Celery	Sweetcorn
Courgettes and marrows	Tomato
Cucumbers	Turnip

Start peppers off in the greenhouse (see p145)

PLANTS TO BE STARTED OFF IN THE GREENHOUSE

Bedding plants

Ageratum	Mimulus
Alyssum	Mesembryanthemum
Antirrhinum	Nemesia
Arabis	Nicotiana
Begonia	Pelargonium
Calceolaria	Perilla
Centaurea	Petunia
Columnea	Salvia
Gazania	Tagetes
Heliotropium	Tropaeolum
Impatiens	Verbena
Lobelia	Zinnia

Begonia 'Can Can' (see p55)

Pelargonium 'Attar of Roses' (see p119)

Gardener's Calendar

The boxes on this spread, detailing the various seasons, provide an overall look at the gardening tasks throughout the year that can be undertaken in the conservatory or greenhouse. However, it is only a guide and you should check entries on individual plants for other seasonal jobs.

Spring

This can be the busiest season in the greenhouse and conservatory, as seed sowing and other propagation is at its peak and require constant attention. You will need to closely monitor the weather in case of frosts and should expect to provide some heating through most of early and mid-spring. Towards the end of spring insulation needs to be removed so that plants receive the maximum light available.

- **In cool greenhouses, continue providing heating in case of late frosts**
- **Open ventilators and windows on warm days**
- **Sow bedding and early vegetable plants for indoors**
- **Sow bedding and early vegetable plants for planting out**
- **Take softwood cuttings**
- **Look out for pests and diseases beginning to move in, and take immediate action**
- **Increase watering and start feeding**
- **Start occasional damping down**
- **Remove insulation as weather warms**
- **Pot on or top dress display plants**

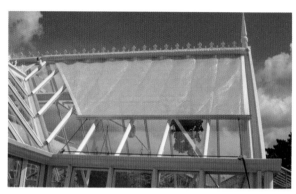

Summer

All systems are go in summer. Watering and damping down are the main jobs needed to keep plants growing well and you will need to do these jobs at least once a day and more in hot weather. There may be a chance to tidy the greenhouse and conservatory up a little as tender bedding and vegetable plants are moved outside.

- **Heating no longer needed**
- **Make sure all outdoor bedding and vegetable plants are planted out**
- **Damping down to be carried out at least once a day**
- **Shading should be in place, particularly on hot days**
- **Open ventilators in warm weather, and open windows and even doors when temperatures really get high**
- **Water daily, sometimes more**
- **Feed all plants regularly**
- **Deadhead flowering plants regularly to encourage more flowers**
- **Train plants while growth is still fairly young and pliable**
- **Take semi-ripe cuttings**
- **Hand pollinate tomatoes, cucumbers and melons**

Spring is the time for sowing and potting on seedlings

Autumn

This is the time of year when you will reap the rewards of your greenhouse or conservatory, especially if you are growing edible plants that are now ready for harvest. It is also a good time to have a clear out to prevent pests and diseases from over wintering, and to carry out any routine maintenance. Prepare for winter by checking heating systems and putting insulation in place.

- **Bring frost-sensitive plants inside to over winter**
- **Harvest fruits and vegetables**
- **Prune and remove any dead or dying growth**
- **Reduce watering and feeding**
- **Ventilate occasionally, during warm spells of weather if possible**
- **Damp down occasionally**
- **Shading should be removed/washed off**
- **Some heating required for cool greenhouses in case of frosts**
- **Carry out autumn cleaning**
- **Check for broken panes**
- **Check for broken guttering**
- **Put insulation into place**
- **Paint softwood greenhouse frames with a wood preservative every few years**

Winter

This is a fairly quiet time in the greenhouse and conservatory as many plants have gone into dormancy. However, if you have frost-sensitive plants, you will need to provide heating throughout winter to keep frosts at bay. You will also need to make sure the area is ventilated regularly to prevent a build up of moisture and disease. Spend some time planning the year ahead.

- **Heating required throughout winter**
- **Cut back almost completely on watering so that plants go into their winter rest**
- **Very few plants will require feeding**
- **Spend some time looking through catalogues and ordering seeds**
- **Do not damp down as a moist atmosphere in winter can encourage disease**
- **On warmer days open ventilators a little to change air**
- **Plant fruit trees such as apricot or peach**

Begin to put insualtion in place during the autumn months

On warmer winter days, open ventilation slats to have a change of air in the greenhouse

Conservatory & Greenhouse Plants

Ornamental plants are the mainstay of the conservatory. While greenhouse gardeners are often most concerned with growing edibles, the conservatory is the place where your imagination can let rip and you can concern yourself with plants of pure ornament.

Edibles can also be grown in a conservatory, but unlike a greenhouse, the main point is to create a human comfort zone where you can be surrounded by all the plants you love. Likewise, there is no reason at all why a greenhouse should not be used in the same way as a conservatory; often positioned some way from the house, they can be an even more private hideaway from the world. As long as you are able to provide heat and water, and somewhere to sit and enjoy the plants, your greenhouse can become a sort of detached conservatory, and can be filled with ornamentals.

Choose plants that will enjoy the conditions you can provide. If you are unsure of your temperature range, it is important to look at the practical section of this book and to decide before you start buying plants. Plants will struggle if they are grown in the wrong temperature. The care table in each entry of the A-Z section will tell you whether each plant is best suited to cold, cool, warm or hot house conditions. Don't worry if you do not have the budget to heat your conservatory to hot house conditions; there is plenty to choose from and you will still find many plants that will help you to create whatever look you are after.

When choosing plants, make sure you use their differing habits to your advantage, to make the fullest possible use of your conservatory or greenhouse. Use specimen plants to make a big impact, evergreens to give backbone, climbers to clothe the walls and roof, and flowering plants to fill in and provide bursts of colour and interest. Whichever plants you choose, this directory will give you the practical advice to ensure they grow happily and healthily.

Abutilon

Abutilons are showy, simple to grow plants, which easily add a tropical feel to any conservatory or greenhouse. As long as the temperature can be kept above 7°C (45°F), they should prove easy to care for.

Abutilon 'Kentish Belle'

Abutilons throw out long, lax stems from which hang brightly coloured flowers. The flowers are roughly bell shaped, and usually come in shades of red, orange and yellow. They are not just grown for their flowers – the foliage is also varied and interesting. The basic shape of the leaf is similar to that of a maple, but many have deeply cut or more rounded shapes to the leaves. There is also a great amount of variegation available, including striking cultivars that have bold, yellow variegation around the edges of the leaves. *Abutilon* 'Cannington Red' is popular for its deep red flowers and foliage that is speckled and splashed with gold spots.

These plants are easy to care for. They can be grown without pruning, if you have lots of space to fill. However, to make sure you have bushy, full plants in summer, cut them back to about half in spring, just before

Abutilon megapotanicum

soil	Any well-drained compost or in a greenhouse or conservatory border
temp	Cool house conditions are suitable if a minimum 7°C (45°F) is maintained
water & humidity	Average watering and humidity required. Water well during summer and carefully during winter
general care	In spring, prune the previous year's growth back by roughly half to encourage bushy growth in summer
pests & diseases	Can suffer from pests such as whitefly, greenfly, scale insects, mealy bugs and red spider mite

growth restarts. This will encourage side shoots to grow. During summer, you will extend the plant's display if you remove any dead flower heads regularly. Plants will need feeding once each month during summer. Take care not to over water in winter, when very little moisture is needed. To propagate, take cuttings in mid-summer or sow seed at 15–18°C (59–64°F) in spring.

As well as being grown as a year-round conservatory or greenhouse plant, abutilons are useful to add height and drama to outdoor summer bedding displays. They should be planted in a sunny spot that is sheltered from strong winds. Only plant them out when all danger of frost has passed, and be careful to bring them in in autumn before cold weather arrives.

	SPRING	SUMMER	AUTUMN	WINTER	height (cm)	spread (cm)	flower colour	
Abutilon 'Cannington Red'		❁ ❁ ❁			200	200	■	Has speckled golden variegation on leaves
A. 'Kentish Belle'		❁ ❁ ❁	❁		250	250	▢	Flowers are often produced into autumn
A. *megapotanicum*		❁ ❁ ❁			100	100	▦	Plant has compact and slightly trailing habit

❁ *flowering*

Acacia

Mimosa *or* Silver wattle

There are few more delicious smells than that of an acacia tree in full bloom. The scent is produced by large numbers of small, fluffy balls of yellow flowers that open in late winter and continue to flourish into spring.

Acacia dealbata

Sprays of the flowers can often be bought in florist's shops in early winter where they go under the common name of mimosa.

They are not plants that have a need for a great deal of heat, and in fact they can occasionally be grown out of doors in temperate climates. It is possible that they may survive in a cold house with no heat at all, as long as they are kept fairly dry over winter.

However, to be sure of success, keep them in a cool house at a minimum temperature of 4°C (39°F) and make sure they are getting temperatures of 16–27°C (61–81°F) in summer, when the flowers are forming. They

soil	Well-drained, multi-purpose compost, or in a greenhouse or conservatory border
temp	Cool house conditions are suitable as a minimum of 4°C (39°F) is required
water & humidity	Water well during summer and sparingly during winter. Little else is required regarding watering
general care	*Acacia dealbata* can grow very large so prune back each spring to prevent it out-growing its space
pests & diseases	Suffers from being attacked by scale insects and red spider mites. Yellow leaves suggest low temperature

Acacia dealbata

do have a need for a great deal of light, and they should be positioned where they will get as much as possible.

The best sized acacia for the average conservatory or greenhouse is *Acacia armata*, the kangaroo thorn. This has thorny stems and yellow flowers and grows to around 3m (10ft) in the wild. It can be kept even smaller in a container.

However, it is *A. dealbata*, the silver wattle, that produces the beautifully scented flowers. This grows extremely large, up to 30m (100ft) in height if left unpruned, so will need cutting back every spring after the flowers have faded if you are to keep it under control. Do not let it grow large and then try to cut it back, as it does not respond well to hard pruning. It also has lovely silvery foliage that folds up at night. Both types should be fed occasionally over summer.

	SPRING	SUMMER	AUTUMN	WINTER	height (cm)	spread (cm)	flower colour	
Acacia armata	● ●				● ●	300	300		Smaller, more manageable plant
A. dealbata	● ●				● ●	1500	600		A large plant but with beautifully scented flowers

● *flowering*

Adiantum capillus-veneris

Maidenhair fern

Adiantum, the maidenhair fern, is an extremely pretty and delicate foliage plant. Its fine, arching black stems carry tiny rounded leaflets, which start life pale green or pale pink and mature to a bright mid-green hue.

Adiantum capillus-veneris

Adiantum capillus-veneris is the classic maidenhair fern. It can be grown in fairly cool conditions, making it ideal for the greenhouse. It is an extremely useful plant for placing with other, flowering plants, as its fuzz of delicate leaves provides the perfect fresh green foil for many flowers. They look particularly good grown together with orchids, which also share their love of moist conditions.

There are a number of different species and cultivars of Adiantum, including some with even smaller, more delicate leaflets, and some with unusual, pink colouring to the young foliage. However, some require more heat than *A. capillus-veneris* and so may not be suitable for growing in cool greenhouse conditions. Make sure of this before you buy.

Ferns generally, and particularly the maidenhair fern, are the sort of plants that are definitely for people who enjoy nurturing, as they will really suffer if neglected. Because the leaflets are so delicate, *A. capillus-veneris* needs constant humidity. Dry air will cause its leaves to turn brown at the edges and for some fronds to eventually die back completely. Allowing the compost to dry out

has much the same effect. It should be moist but not sodden at all times. Damping down in the greenhouse or conservatory will certainly help to raise the humidity but it may be a good idea to regularly mist the leaves of Adiantum plants and to place a pebble tray or saucer of moist expanded clay granules under or near the plant. They should be grown among or beneath other humidity-loving plants so that a moist miniature microclimate is created. They do like to be grown in fairly bright conditions, but should always be kept in filtered light

soil	Well-drained, multi-purpose compost, or in a greenhouse or conservatory border
temp	Average temperatures of between 16–27°C (61–81°F). Minimum 4°C (39°F)
water & humidity	Lots of water in growing season. Water sparingly in winter. Needs high humidity, so mist regularly
general care	Regularly remove dead fronds right down to the base of the plant. This will encourage new ones to grow
pests & diseases	Scale insects and mealy bugs. Fronds turn brown and die if the compost or the air around the plant is dry

where possible, and should always be shaded from the direct rays of midday summer sun. While the plant is in active growth during spring and summer, apply a half-strength liquid fertilizer once a month to encourage new fronds to form.

On the bottom of the leaflets there are small brown patches. These are where the spores are produced by which means ferns propagate. They are not a sign of disease, for which they can be mistaken. Propagating from spores is tricky and a simpler way to increase stock is to divide the rhizome and replant sections of it in fresh compost in early spring.

Aeschynanthus radicans
Lipstick vine

Aeschynanthus is a genus of plants that are popular as houseplants. They need warm conditions to grow well and so are best grown in a greenhouse that is kept at hothouse temperatures all year round, or in a conservatory that is kept at normal house temperatures. Alternatively they can be grown in a greenhouse over summer, where the high light levels will encourage a great display of flowers, and then moved into the house over winter.

Aeschynanthus radicans is more often sold as *A. lobbianus*. It is the most widely grown of the genus and is popular for its trailing stems clothed in pairs of fresh green leaves and bearing bright red, almost scarlet, tube-shaped flowers. It is commonly known as the lipstick vine because of this vibrant colouring. Due to their trailing habit, lipstick vines make excellent specimens for use in hanging baskets. They can flower from summer right through to winter, so they provide their splashes of bright colour for most of the year. Although good light levels will encourage flowering, try to provide filtered light and some shade from direct summer sun.

They originate in subtropical forests, and the best soil for them is a mixture of peat and sphagnum moss. This should be kept moist at all times throughout the growing season, as their need for water is fairly high. Use soft water if possible. If you live in a hard water area, then it is a good idea to

soil	Compost made of fibrous peat and sphagnum moss. Suitable for hanging basket
temp	Minimum temperatures of 15–18°C (59–64°F). Suitable for hot house conditions
water & humidity	Water well, using soft water, during growing season; sparingly in winter. High humidity, so mist regularly
general care	Cuttings can be taken in spring, but rooting is slow so use a propagator with bottom heat
pests & diseases	Aphids can sometimes cause problems on the young growth. Otherwise fairly trouble free

collect rainwater to water these plants, rather than using the hard water that comes out of the tap. It should be collected in a bowl or bucket and used as soon as possible. Do not use rainwater that has been sitting in butts for a long time, as this may be harbouring pests and diseases that will harm the plants.

Aeschynanthus also need high levels of humidity, so should be misted regularly and placed in an area of the greenhouse or conservatory that is regularly damped down and in which other plants that love high humidity are grouped. You could also place the container in a tray of expanded clay granules. These should be kept moist at all times and water will then gradually evaporate so that it keeps the area around the leaves humid.

In winter, reduce watering but still water occasionally, so that the compost does not get too dry. Humidity should also be lowered during winter to prevent moulds and rots from having a chance to develop.

Aeschynanthus radicans

Agave

Agave americana and its cultivars are impressive succulents that make perfect conservatory or greenhouse plants. They look good surrounded by the quirky shapes of other cacti and succulents.

Agave americana

They need lots of space and light, and given these conditions they will grow into their full, spiky, sculptural rosette. *Agave americana* is larger and plain green and *A. americana* 'Mediopicta' has a thick pale yellow stripe down the centre of the leaf. It grows slower and stays smaller than the all green species, so is often easier to grow if space is at all confined. In temperate climates, agaves can be moved out of doors during summer.

Agaves are known as century plants, as they can take many years to flower, although not nearly as many as a hundred. They will usually flower within 10 years. After they flower, the flowering rosette will die, but this is not too much of a problem as small offsets appear at the sides of the main plant at about this time, and these can be removed and potted on to grow into full-sized plants.

The real benefit of growing these plants in a greenhouse or conservatory is that it keeps winter rain away from them. Agaves can sometimes tolerate quite low temperatures as long as they are dry, and it is wet weather combined with low temperatures that usually kills them if they are grown out of doors over winter in temperate climates.

Water carefully in summer and allow to rest in winter, keeping the plant almost completely dry. Agaves do not require high humidity, so position them among a group of other plants that do not need to be regularly misted.

Look out for pests such as scale insects that can attack the undersides of the leaves, as well as the young growth at the centre of the plant.

Agave americana 'Mediopicta'

soil	Grow in cacti and succulent compost that includes some grit to ensure good drainage
temp	Minimum temperature 4°C (39°F). Cool greenhouse, can be put outdoors in summer
water & humidity	Water sparingly while actively growing. Keep almost dry in winter while resting. Low humidity
general care	Main rosette dies after flowering, pot up the small offshoots that arise at base of plant into fresh compost
pests & diseases	Scale insects can attack plants, particularly young growth. Wilting is often caused by over watering

	SPRING	SUMMER	AUTUMN	WINTER	height (cm)	spread (cm)	leaf colour	
Agave americana		● ● ●			100	180		Strong shape and spiny leaf edges
A. americana 'Mediopicta'		● ● ●			100	150		Central yellow stripe to leaves

● *flowering*

A

Allamanda cathartica

Golden trumpet vine

Allamanda cathartica is commonly known as the golden trumpet vine. It is a beautiful, vigorous plant that produces huge, trumpet-shaped, bold yellow flowers throughout summer and autumn. Originally from tropical forests of North and South America, its exotic flowers will bring a touch of the tropics to any conservatory.

Considering that it produces such an impressive display, this plant is relatively easy to care for, and not at all temperamental as long as it is given the correct amount of warmth and humidity.

It is a large climber, and can grow up to 16m (52ft) high in the wild. In a greenhouse or conservatory it will obviously not reach these heights. However, it will need space to grow and is at its best if it is allowed the free root run afforded by being planted in a greenhouse or conservatory border. If you are growing it in a pot, it will need to be a particularly large one at least 36cm (14in) across and larger if possible. It is best to restrict its height by pruning every year in winter. If you want to keep the plant fairly small, cut it right back nearly to the ground, just leaving a couple of buds from which the new growth will sprout. If you are trying to grow the plant to fill a large space, it is still a good idea to prune once a year in winter but remove only about half of the growth. This will help to keep the plant bushy and prevent legginess by encouraging shoots to grow from the base of the plant. Take care when pruning, as the sap can irritate the skin and is likely to cause an upset stomach

soil	Multi-purpose compost. Often best when planted in a greenhouse	
temp	Minimum temperatures of 7°C (45°F). Grow in cool or warm greenhouse conditions	
water & humidity	Water well when in growth and then sparingly in autumn and winter. Requires high humidity	
general care	Prune in winter to keep the plant down to size or to keep the base of it bushy. Little else is required	
pests & diseases	Whiteflies can attack plants and red-spider mite can be a problem, particularly in conditions of low humidity	

if it is accidentally eaten. Wear gloves while pruning and wash your hands immediately afterwards.

You will need to provide good sturdy supports for the plant to grow up. A strong trellis attached to a wall is suitable, as is a series of horizontal wires, attached with vine eyes. It is such a large climber that it can look good trained along the ridge of a greenhouse or conservatory, from where the yellow flower will hang down. Wherever it is grown, tie shoots in loosely throughout the season as they appear, in order to keep the plant tidy and to stop it from taking up too much space.

To propagate Allamanda, take cuttings in spring or early summer.

Allamanda cathartica

Androsace

Androsace may seem a strange candidate for growing in a greenhouse, as it is completely hardy. In fact, it is one of a group of plants that need protection not from the cold, but from the wet of the average winter.

Androsace ciliata

greenhouse (these plants are completely unsuited to conservatories) will need to be unheated all year round and should have particularly good ventilation. As well as installing extra ventilators, it can be a good idea to fit a fan that will keep air moving in the greenhouse in warmer weather. This will help keep the air cool. Keep doors and ventilators open at all times, except in particularly rough weather. Greenhouses can be a little warm for these plants in summer, and so it is a good idea to provide some shading. You can also move the plants outside in summer, as they can cope with rainfall when they are actively growing.

Grow them in a well-drained soil and place grit on the surface of the compost, around the base of the plant, to prevent the leaves from sitting on wet compost. Water the plants from below if possible, to prevent the crowns from getting too wet.

These plants are alpines – plants that grow high up mountain sides where they are exposed to extremely low temperatures, but are covered up by a layer of frozen snow all winter so that they receive almost no moisture at all until the snow melts in spring. In winters in temperate climates, if grown outside the roots of these plants would simply rot away. Not all alpines are so sensitive to wet and many can be grown out of doors, but there are a select few that can only be successfully grown under cover and Androsace is among them.

To grow them well you will really need to set up an alpine house, in which case you will be able to grow many other alpines, but few types of other greenhouse plants as there will not be enough heat for them. The

soil	An alpine compost of half potting compost, half grit. Cover the surface with grit
temp	Androsace are completely hardy and will need no heat at all to grow well
water & humidity	Water well when in growth and then sparingly in the autumn and winter. Requires low humidity
general care	Good ventilation is needed to keep these plants healthy. Install extra ventilators and leave doors open often
pests & diseases	Aphids can occasionally be a problem. Moist conditions, particularly in winter, can lead to rots developing

	SPRING	SUMMER	AUTUMN	WINTER	height (cm)	spread (cm)	flower colour	
Androsace ciliata	● ●				2.5	8	▓	Pretty pink flowers held above a mound of foliage
A. vandellii	● ●				5	12	☐	Forms a dense cushion of rosettes

● flowering

Anigozanthos
Kangaroo paw

Anigozanthus is commonly known as the kangaroo paw. This is because of the strange shapes of the flowers, which are covered in many tiny hairs and so resemble small, furry paws.

Unsurprisingly, given this common name, the plant originates in Australia. It makes an exotic and unusual addition to a cool greenhouse.

Greenhouses and conservatories are useful in opening up a range of cut flowers that cannot be grown in the garden, and Anigozanthos must be the most exciting of all of these. Their stiff, solid blooms make brilliant cut flowers that are particularly long lasting and have an unusual shape and texture. They cannot easily be grown out of doors in temperate climates, but this is more because of excessive winter wet than because of low temperatures, and so they can be grown in a cool greenhouse as long as they are kept fairly dry during winter. In fact, *Anigozanthos manglesii* will survive

Anigozanthos flavidus

soil	Grows best in a well-drained compost with plenty of organic matter incorporated
temp	Grow in cool house conditions with a minimum temperature of 5°C (41°F)
water & humidity	Water well in spring and summer when in growth and then keep almost totally dry in winter
general care	Needs high levels of light and will take some direct sun. Feed once a month during the growing season
pests & diseases	Generally these plants are fairly trouble free, although they can suffer from a form of leaf spot

Anigozanthos flavidus

outdoors if it is mulched well before winter, but you are likely to get far better and more predictable results growing it in a cool greenhouse that is kept frost-free. Plants should receive good levels of light, including some direct sunlight, particularly in summer when they are actively growing.

Plant up into a compost containing large amounts of leaf mould or soil if possible. Anigozanthos enjoys fairly high levels of organic matter. They can be grown from seed or from division, but the plant is sensitive to disturbance and divided roots can take a while to settle down. Take care when propagating by division, as the roots are fleshy and easily broken.

A. flavidus is a fairly large plant, growing up to 3m (10ft) in height in the wild, but less in cultivation if grown in a container. *A. manglesii* is a far more compact and manageable plant.

	SPRING	SUMMER	AUTUMN	WINTER	height (cm)	spread (cm)	flower colour	
Anigozanthos flavidus		● ● ●			100	60		Large plant producing green to red flowers
A. manglesii	● ● ●	●			60	40		Compact plant, good for cut flowers

● flowering

Aphelandra squarrosa 'Louisae'

Aphelandra would most probably be a popular plant for its foliage alone. The fact that it also produces beautifully showy flowers adds to its value as a conservatory or greenhouse plant.

The foliage of *Aphelandra squarrosa* 'Louisae', the most frequently grown of the genus, is large, glossy and dark green. It is marked by bold contrasting veins that are almost white in colour. The flowers are usually produced in autumn but can appear throughout the year. They consist primarily of a cone of waxy, bright yellow bracts, edged in red, which can grow up to 10cm (4in) long. From within these bracts are produced more ephemeral yellow flowers. The bracts are strong and long lasting, often providing up to six weeks of colour.

Aphelandra will survive at temperatures down to -7°C (19°F). However, to really thrive it needs higher temperatures. This makes a cool greenhouse unsuitable, but plants will do well grown in a conservatory, or in a warm greenhouse. Soil needs to be rich in organic matter, and so it is a good idea to mix some leaf mould into the potting mix.

Aphelandra squarrosa 'Louisae'

Aphelandra plants originate in damp, tropical woodlands and leaf mould will help to recreate their native conditions. Throughout summer, plants should be watered well with soft water. If you live in a hard-water area, avoid using tap water and instead collect fresh rainwater in a clean container. Use this immediately to avoid any build up of pests or diseases in the water. If you live in a soft-water area, you will be able to water the plants using tap water. In winter, continue to use soft water, but reduce watering. Apply a liquid fertilizer every fortnight during summer. You should continue feeding throughout winter, but less frequently.

In order to keep the plant looking compact and bushy, you will need to prune it regularly. However, if you do this at the wrong time, you might cut off developing flower spikes. Wait until flowering is over and then cut the plant back at the same time as you remove the old flowers. Cut back fairly hard and make sure that the cut is just above the point where leaves emerge from the stem. If you have not carried out any pruning by early spring, this is a good time to do it, as new growth will soon appear.

Flowering will be best if plants are kept in good light, although you should be careful to shade them from the heat of the midday sun during summer.

soil	Grows best in a well-drained compost with some leaf mould incorporated
temp	Grow in warm greenhouse conditions with a minimum temperature of 7°C (45°F)
water & humidity	Water well with soft water when in active growth and cut down on watering in winter
general care	Cut the stems back hard in spring to encourage fresh growth and a compact, bushy shape
pests & diseases	Mealy bugs, scale insects and aphids can all cause problems. Aphids attack new growing tips

Araucaria heterophylla

Norfolk Island pine

Araucaria heterophylla is a useful conservatory or greenhouse plant that provides fresh green ferny foliage. It is good as a standard plant in its own right, but also creates a lovely foil for flowering plants to show themselves off against.

Norfolk Island pine's natural home is on this small island in the Pacific Ocean. It is related to the well-known monkey-puzzle tree and in its natural environment will grow up to 45m (150ft) in height. But do not panic; it will grow to nothing like these dimensions in a greenhouse situation. In fact, it is fairly easy to keep at a manageable size of around 2m (6ft) in height. It is best grown in a pot and kept slightly pot bound, as this helps to restrict the size. Do not plant it out into a conservatory or greenhouse border because it is then likely to put on a lot more growth than you will have the space for.

Araucaria heterophylla is really a tree, consisting of a central stem, clothed in green needles, from which emerge several tiers of foliage. These are held horizontally

soil	Moist, freely draining compost. Grows too large if planted in greenhouse border
temp	Grow in cool greenhouse conditions with a minimum temperature of 4°C (39°F)
water & humidity	Water normally when in active growth and then sparingly in winter. Requires good levels of humidity
general care	Should be potted on into a slightly bigger pot only every 3–4 years to prevent it growing too large
pests & diseases	Leaf drop and yellowing can be caused by low humidity and high levels of heat and light in summer

from the central stem and are covered in the fine, bright green needles. New growth is a lovely fresh green.

A. heterophylla will suffer if kept in conditions that are too warm and bright, so if growing in a conservatory, it will have to be kept at a fairly cool temperature. In hot, dry, bright conditions the foliage will start to turn yellow and may drop. It is happiest in fairly high humidity and with good ventilation, particularly on hot summer days.

It looks good grouped with ferns, which enjoy the same levels of humidity and well-filtered summer light. It will, however, enjoy higher light levels in winter. Water fairly well in summer and then keep compost almost dry in winter. This mirrors the plant's natural environment, in which there is a long dry season. Feeding should be every two weeks in summer with a liquid fertilizer and should be stopped in winter.

Pruning can be carried out if the plant is becoming too large, but it can be tricky to avoid ruining the shape of the plant, so it is better to take steps to restrict the growth to avoid this problem. If you do need to prune, the best time is at the end of summer.

Araucaria heterophylla

Araucaria heterophylla

Begonia

There are a great number of begonias that make good conservatory and greenhouse plants. Begonias come in all shapes, sizes and colours. Some have big, blousy, brightly coloured blooms while others have more delicate, subtle flowers. They are easy to care for and there is one for every taste.

There are several groups of begonias and each has its own maintenance needs. Those begonias that grow from tubers, such as *Begonia* 'Can Can' and *B.* 'Pin Up', will need to be planted up each spring. Keep the tubers warm and water carefully until a few shoots show. Increase watering as the plant grows and then water more freely while the plant is flowering. Feed every month from the beginning of

soil	Begonias will grow best when planted in a moist, freely draining compost
temp	Grow in warm greenhouse conditions with a minimum temperature of 10°C (50°F)
water & humidity	Water well when in active growth and then sparingly in winter. Require high levels of humidity in summer
general care	Should be potted on every year. Tubers will need drying out in winter and replanting in spring
pests & diseases	Mealy bugs, thrips, vine weevils, aphids, grey mould, powdery mildew and stem rot can all attack plants

Begonia 'Can Can'

flowering until the foliage dies back. Provide high humidity on hot summer days by frequent misting of the leaves. The fleshy stems of begonias are susceptible to rots, so it is important not to over water at any time. After flowering, you will need to reduce watering until the foliage dies down. Cut the dead foliage away, dry out the

tubers, then clean them and store them in a dry place until it is time for planting out the following spring.

There are many winter-flowering begonias that can provide a splash of colour at an otherwise dull time of year. These, which include such plants as *B.* 'Azotus', will not die back like the tuberous begonias. Throughout winter, put them in the brightest spot you have to encourage flowering. Some people find it easiest to throw these plants out after flowering and to simply buy new ones the following year. However, they are fairly straightforward to keep alive if you water carefully throughout summer.

All begonias are easy to propagate from leaf cuttings taken in spring. See the 'Propagation' section (p38) for details.

	SPRING	SUMMER	AUTUMN	WINTER	height (cm)	spread (cm)	flower colour	
Begonia 'Azotus'				☀ ☀ ☀	20	15	▮	Glossy, dark green leaves and vibrant flowers
B. 'Can Can'	🌱	☀ ☀ ☀			90	45	▯	Good upright shape to plant
B. 'Love me'				☀ ☀ ☀	45	25	▮	Pretty, single flowers borne throughout winter
B. 'Pin Up'	🌱	☀ ☀ ☀			25	20	▯	Extremely free flowering

🌱 *planting*   ☀ *flowering*

Bougainvillea

Huge bougainvilleas are seen in abundance in areas with Mediterranean climates, but it is easy for those in more temperate climes to grow them in a greenhouse or conservatory. They are large and vigorous and will be clothed in bold colour throughout summer and into autumn.

The colourful 'flowers' are in fact large, papery, petal-like bracts. The true flowers are produced from the centres of these bracts and are fairly insignificant. Plants are available with bracts in almost all of the colours of the rainbow. There are also plants with interesting, variegated leaves, which act as a good foil for the bright flowers.

They like a good root run and so are perfect subjects for planting out in a conservatory or greenhouse border. If this is not possible, make sure you plant them in as big a pot as possible. They will grow to a large size in these situations, but are happy to be cut back hard in autumn or winter and this will keep them in check and stop them from taking over. Spur pruning

soil	Grow best in freely draining compost or in a conservatory or greenhouse border
temp	Grow in warm greenhouse conditions with a minimum temperature of 7°C (45°F)
water & humidity	Water well in active growth and when flowering and then carefully in winter. Mist occasionally in hot weather
general care	Prune every year in winter, shorten vegetative growth to encourage formation of short, floriferous spurs
pests & diseases	Mealy bugs, red spider mite, scale insect and whitefly can all cause problems on bougainvillea plants

will encourage more flowers. This means shortening the previous year's long side shoots to about a third of their length. Growth that is then put on the following season is not as soft and sappy, and is more likely to bear flowers.

To encourage flowering, grow plants in full sun all year round. During flowering and active growth, they should be watered freely and fed every month. They will need misting when the weather is particularly warm in summer. In winter, reduce watering and keep just moist. Top dress plants in spring with fresh compost or pot on if possible.

It is possible to propagate bougainvillea from cuttings taken in summer, if you are able to provide a little bottom heat by starting them off in a heated propagator.

Bougainvillea glabra 'Snow White'

	SPRING	SUMMER	AUTUMN	WINTER	height (cm)	spread (cm)	flower colour	
Bougainvillea x buttiana 'Louise Wathen'		● ● ●	● ● ●		1000	400		Vigorous plant with bright orange bracts
B. glabra		● ● ●	● ● ●		800	300		The species from which most available plants are bred
B. glabra 'Snow White'		● ● ●	● ● ●		800	300		Evergreen leaves and white flowers

● *flowering*

Bouvardia

Bouvardia is a long-flowering plant that can produce its delicate blooms from late summer right through until early winter. It loves conservatory and greenhouse conditions because it needs good amounts of light to flower really well.

Bouvardia ternifolia

The flowers of *Bouvardia longiflora* are fine, slender and white in appearance, and are pleasantly scented. They hang down delicately from the branches. Those of *B. ternifolia* are bright red in colour.

They are at their best when grown in cool or warm greenhouse conditions or in a conservatory. If grown well they can be almost completely covered in their small, tubular flowers over a long period. Few flowers will be produced if the plant is kept in a shady spot, so ensure good light throughout summer. Keep shaded from the heat of the midday sun in mid-summer. Good winter light is also important.

One of the problems with these plants is that they can grow leggy. They will need cutting back hard in early spring before growth starts and then should have their tips pinched out regularly. This will encourage shoots to form along the stems of the plant and will help it to develop into a more bushy shape. Stop pinching out when flowers start to appear or you will remove buds.

At the height of summer, plants will need a little extra humidity, so mist them regularly, especially in warm weather and group them with other plants that enjoy higher levels of humidity. Feeding is only really necessary once a month throughout summer. Water well throughout summer, but cut back on watering towards winter until the compost is kept not quite dry, with just an occasional dribble of water.

Cuttings can be attempted in summer, but are unlikely to take unless you are able to provide some bottom heat from a heated propagator.

soil	Bouvardias will grow best if grown in a good, multi-purpose compost
temp	Grow in cool or warm greenhouse conditions, minimum 5°C (41°F)
water & humidity	Water well in active growth during the growing season, and sparingly in winter. High humidity in summer
general care	Plants can grow leggy, so regularly pinch out the tips to encourage them to grow into a good, bushy shape
pests & diseases	Mealy bugs, red spider mite and whitefly can all cause problems on Bouvardia plants

	SPRING	SUMMER	AUTUMN	WINTER	height (cm)	spread (cm)	flower colour	
Bouvardia longiflora			● ● ● ●	●	80	60	☐	Bears fragrant white flowers
B. ternifolia			● ● ● ●	●	70	50	■	Scarlet flowers borne over a long season

● flowering

Brugmansia
Datura

If you are looking for a showy and dramatic plant for your greenhouse or conservatory, look no further than Brugmansia. This is the plant formerly – and widely – known as datura. It produces huge, trumpet-shaped flowers that add a tropical note to any conservatory.

What makes brugmansia so impressive is the size of its flowers and leaves. The flowers can grow up to 30cm (12in) long and the hairy, green leaves can each reach a length of 60cm (24in). The plant itself can also grow extremely large, so it is essential to keep it in check. However, the plant will grow best if given a free root run and will not reward attempts to keep it down to size by allowing it to get pot bound. The best way to treat it is to give it a large pot, or even to plant it out into your greenhouse or conservatory border, and then to prune it back hard every winter. New growth will soon appear and in no time the plant will be making its presence felt. If they are grown in a pot they can be moved out of doors during summer when there is no chance of frost.

Some of the loveliest of the brugmansias are those with scented blooms. *Brugmansia x candida* produces scented pale yellow or white flowers. The scent is at its strongest

Brugmansia x candida 'Variegata'

soil	Grows well in multi-purpose compost. Can be planted into greenhouse
temp	Grow in warm greenhouse conditions with a minimum temperature of 7°C (45°F)
water & humidity	Water well while in active growth during the growing season and sparingly in winter. Average humidity
general care	Brugmansias can grow large, cut them back hard each winter to stop them taking up too much space
pests & diseases	Mealy bugs and whitefly can all cause problems. Red spider mite can be a problem if humidity is low in summer

in the evening and at night. *B. suaveolens* is also strongly scented at night and has white flowers.

Brugmansia suaveolens

These plants need a position in good light, all year round. They should be watered well during the growing season and their compost kept slightly moist in winter. They should be fed about once a month during the spring and summer.

Do not grow brugmansia if you have small children or pets, as parts of the plant are highly poisonous.

	SPRING	SUMMER	AUTUMN	WINTER	height (cm)	spread (cm)	flower colour	
Brugmansia x candida		● ● ●	● ●		400	200		Flowers are scented at night
B. sanguinea	●	● ● ●	● ●		500	250		Long, trumpet shaped yellow flowers with red tips
B. suaveolens		● ● ●	● ●		500	250		Flowers are sometimes tinged with pink

● *flowering*

Callistemon
Bottlebrush

Callistemon is an unusual but extremely attractive Australian shrub. It bears fluffy, brightly coloured brushes of flowers around the tips of its stems in summer. The really strange effect is produced later, however, as the stem peeps out of the end of the flower and continues to grow.

They make great greenhouse and cool conservatory plants as they really need little winter heat to keep them happy. They are also pretty compact plants and can be kept smaller than the measurements given here by keeping them in fairly small containers – their eventual size will be determined by the size of the pot they are in. Direct planting into greenhouse and conservatory borders suits them, but they will grow into larger shrubs than they would in pots. Whether in a pot or in a border they will produce huge amounts of flowers for their relatively compact size.

Callistemons can be pruned back fairly hard if they do get too large for the space available but this will be at the expense of flowers. All flowers are formed on growth that is at least one year old, so cutting the

Callistemon citrinus

whole shrub back will mean sacrificing a whole year's blooms. If you need to reduce the size, cut about a third of the stems off each year over a few years to avoid this problem. If you do not need to reduce the size, only prune out damaged stems or those that are making the plant look congested or untidy.

These plants do have one definite requirement, and that is for light. They should be in high light levels all year round. Keep them well watered in summer and feed them once a month. Reduce watering and stop feeding in winter. Make sure that they have really good ventilation on hot summer days.

soil	Well-drained, multi-purpose compost. Can be planted into greenhouse
temp	Grow in cool greenhouse conditions with a minimum temperature of 4°C (39°F)
water & humidity	Water well while in active growth during the growing season, and sparingly in winter. Average humidity
general care	Can be pruned back hard if ever necessary, but be aware that flowers are borne on the previous year's growth
pests & diseases	Fairly problem free but mealy bugs, scale insects and red spider mites can all cause problems

	SPRING	SUMMER	AUTUMN	WINTER	height (cm)	spread (cm)	flower colour	
Callistemon citrinus	● ● ●	● ● ●			150	150	■	Extremely floriferous greenhouse shrub
C. 'Mauve Mist'		● ● ●			200	200	▨	Unusual purple colouring to flowers
C. pityoides		● ●			100	100	□	Compact plant bearing yellow flowers

● *flowering*

59

Camellia

Camellias are beautiful shrubs that are often seen growing out of doors quite happily. A sight that is also often seen in early spring is a camellia covered in a mass of brown, ruined flowers, the remains of a once promising display. This is the reason they are grown in conservatories and greenhouses – it is the best way to keep their beautiful and delicate flowers protected from frost.

The problem camellias have is their timing. When their flowers arrive, earlier than any other flowers of their size, frosts are still rife and so many end up being destroyed by frost just as they are getting into their stride.

They make good, easy to care for conservatory and greenhouse plants, and will stay fairly compact if grown in a pot. They are also evergreen and provide a good foil of dark, glossy leaves year round against which to grow other plants. Container growing also allows those who do not live on acid soils to grow camellias, as they are lime haters and will soon turn yellow and sickly if grown in anything other than ericaceous compost.

It is also important to water with soft water to help maintain the acidity of the soil. If you live in a hard-water area this will mean collecting fresh rainwater regularly. They do not need huge amounts of water at any time of year, but water fairly well in

soil	Camellias require ericaceous (lime-free) compost to grow well
temp	Can be grown in cold house; best results grow in a cool house at 4°C (39°F) minimum
water & humidity	Water well, using soft water, while in active growth, and sparingly in winter. Average humidity
general care	Plants can benefit from being moved outdoors into a sheltered spot in dappled shade during the summer
pests & diseases	Scale insects, Aphids and vine weevil. Yellowing often caused by lime-containing compost

spring and summer, and reduce watering in winter. Feed only occasionally, over summer. Heat is not all that important, but it will help if you can keep the greenhouse frost-free over their flowering time.

Camellia reticulata flowers in spring, *C. japonica* in winter and early spring, and *C. sasanqua* from autumn through to spring. There are a huge number of cultivars of each species available, in many different shapes and shades.

Camellia japonica white hybrid

	SPRING	SUMMER	AUTUMN	WINTER	height (cm)	spread (cm)	flower colour	
Camellia japonica	● ●				300	150	■	Species from which many good cultivars have been bred
C. reticulata	● ●			●	500	300	■	Larger shrub with open habit
C. sasanqua	●			● ● ● ●	400	200	□	Can flower in the depths of winter

● *flowering*

Campanula

The genus Campanula includes several plants that are suitable for growing in greenhouses and conservatories. The most popular of these is *Campanula isophylla*, which is grown in normal conservatory conditions or in a cool greenhouse.

It has delicate, tumbling cascades of flowers. Grow it in a hanging basket so that its cascade of flowering stems can be shown off to their full potential. The other plants are alpines, and need the specialist conditions that are provided by an alpine house.

One of the reasons *C. isophylla* is so popular is that it is so easy to grow. Given regular watering and an occasional trim it will produce masses of pretty flowers from early summer through to early autumn. It does need warm summer temperatures, though, or its display can be disappointing.

In winter it is important to keep it in low temperatures and to reduce watering. If given warmth at this time, the plant could start into growth, and this would weaken it for the following season. Be careful not to allow it to become frosted, however, as this may kill the plant.

Campanula isophylla

The alpine campanulas are among a group of plants that need protection not from winter cold, but from winter rain. They naturally grow high up mountainsides where they are exposed to low temperatures, but are covered up by a layer of frozen snow all winter, so receive almost no moisture until spring. Outside, in winters in temperate climates, the roots of these plants rot away.

They should be grown in an alpine house. This is a greenhouse that is unheated all year. As well as installing extra ventilators, fit a fan that will keep air moving in the greenhouse in warmer weather to keep the air cool. Keep doors and ventilators open whenever possible. Greenhouses can get warm in summer, so provide some shading. You can also move the plants outside in summer, as they enjoy rainfall when they are actively growing.

Grow in a gritty, well-drained soil and place grit on the surface of the compost, around the base of the plant. Water them from below.

soil	Grow in multi-purpose compost; *C. lasiocarpa* and *C. raineri* in an alpine mix
temp	Cold house conditions for all except *C. isophylla* (minimum 4°C/39°F)
water & humidity	Water well while in active growth and sparingly in winter. Keep *C. lasiocarpa* and *C. raineri* dry in winter.
general care	Should be well ventilated all year round. Remove flowers as they fade to encourage more to form
pests & diseases	Aphids, red spider mite, vine weevil, powdery mildew. Leaves turn yellow if plant not fed adequately

	SPRING	SUMMER	AUTUMN	WINTER	height (cm)	spread (cm)	flower colour	
Campanula isophylla		✺ ✺ ✺			50	30		Floriferous plant and a good trailer
C. lasiocarpa		✺ ✺ ✺			8	20		Alpine plant producing delicate flowers
C. raineri		✺ ✺ ✺			8	20		Alpine plant producing larger flowers

✺ flowering

Campsis
Trumpet vine

Among the many beautiful and exotic climbers that can be grown in a conservatory or heated greenhouse is Campsis, commonly known as the Chinese trumpet vine. This large climber will quickly fill a conservatory with its fresh green leaves and deep orange coloured, trumpet-shaped flowers.

soil	Grows in any multi-purpose compost if well drained. Incorporate extra grit
temp	Grow campsis in warm or cool greenhouse conditions. Minimum 5°C (41°F)
water & humidity	Water well while in active growth and sparingly in winter. Requires average humidity
general care	Campsis can grow large but will tolerate pruning in late autumn. Create a framework to prune back to
pests & diseases	Aphids, red spider mite, scale insect, powdery mildew, mealy bugs and whitefly all attack plants

The flowers are borne in late summer and autumn. In the most popular form, *Campsis tagliabuana* 'Madame Galen', the flowers emerge a pale coral colour and darken to a deep, burnt orange. *C. radicans* f. *flava* produces yellow flowers. The leaves of both are mid-green, delicate and deciduous.

Although it grows to large dimensions, it is fairly easy to contain by pruning. This should be carried out in late autumn, after the leaves have fallen. Rather than pruning the whole plant back to the ground, create a framework of branches to prune back to each year. Select a few particularly strong shoots to keep and prune back any weaker ones. Any side shoots that have grown on your main shoots can be shortened or removed. Carry this out each year and the plant will remain a manageable size.

Keeping it in a large pot, rather than growing it in a greenhouse border, will also help to prevent it growing too large. Campsis plants need particularly good drainage, and will suffer if their roots sit in cold, damp soil. Improve drainage my mixing horticultural grit into the compost. Place a layer of broken crocks over the bottom of the pot before filling with compost, to prevent the drainage holes from getting clogged up.

Grow in full sun and train against a wall if possible, tying stems into a trellis or set of horizontal wires. Feed occasionally through summer. Propagation is fairly easy, as plants throw up suckers that can be carefully removed when the plant is potted on.

Campsis radicans

	SPRING	SUMMER	AUTUMN	WINTER	height (cm)	spread (cm)	flower colour	
Campsis radicans		● ●	● ● ●		1000	1000	■	Beautiful, reddish-orange flowered climber
Campsis radicans f. flava		● ●	● ● ●		1000	1000	☐	Yellow-flowered form of *C. radicans*
C. tagliabuana 'Madame Galen'		● ●	● ● ●		1000	1000	■	Flowers open pale and darken as they age

● *flowering*

Cattleya

Cattleyas are excellent plants to start off with for the orchid novice. They are easy to grow and flower, yet still have the impressive blooms sought after by orchid growers. Many are also scented.

Cattleya hybrid

soil	Grow in an open, bark-based orchid compost in a hanging basket if possible
temp	Cool or warm greenhouse conditions with a minimum temperature of 5°C (41°F)
water & humidity	Water in summer, letting compost dry out between waterings, and even less in winter. High humidity
general care	Can be propagated by division. Wait until container is completely filled before splitting carefully
pests & diseases	Aphids, red spider mite, scale insect, mealy bugs and grey mould can all attack plants

The flowers consist of five large petals pulled back from a central tube that can be attractively frilled or ruched at the end. Each flowering stem usually holds five or six of these flowers. The leaves and stems arise from swollen stem structures known as pseudobulbs. Cattleyas are good candidates for growing in hanging baskets filled with orchid compost, as the flowers hang down from the plant. If the hanging basket is lined with moss, some stems may even grow out of the base of the basket, creating an even more impressive display of flowers.

Cattleya aclandiae is one of the easiest species of the genus to grow, and is an especially good one to try if you are new to orchid cultivation. *C. bowringiana* is also fairly easy and extremely attractive. Both species flower in the autumn. As well as these, there are many colourful Cattleya cultivars available that are worth experimenting with.

They will do well in a sunny spot and need good bright light all year round, but they should be afforded a little shade from the hottest midday summer sun. They are best kept in warm or cool greenhouse conditions, but place them in a spot where they will receive a little extra ventilation in the autumn.

Humidity should be high at all times, so mist the leaves regularly and place a tray of moist pebbles or expanded clay granules near the container. You could also group them with other humidity lovers such as ferns, which will provide a lovely foil for their flowers. It is important to grow them in an open textured orchid compost. Allow the compost to almost dry out between waterings, and reduce watering in winter and while flowering.

	SPRING	SUMMER	AUTUMN	WINTER	height (cm)	spread (cm)	flower colour	
Cattleya aclandiae			● ● ●		30	20	▮	Good orchid for beginners
C. bowringiana			● ● ●	●	80	35	▮	Deep pink flowers produced in autumn

● *flowering*

Chamaedorea elegans

Parlour palm

All palms make graceful conservatory and greenhouse plants. They grow slowly but will eventually become large enough to make impressive foliage plants. Chamaedorea is easy to care for and will make a good-sized specimen plant once it is a few years old.

Chamaedorea elegans is commonly known as the parlour palm. It has tall, arching leaves that bear a number of smaller leaflets, arranged in pairs up the leaf stalk. Over time plants can grow up to 2m (6½ft) in height and can form a clump up to 1.5m (5ft) across, although it is more likely to reach about 90cm (3ft) across in a pot. Despite their eventual size, they have a refined, elegant appearance. When the plant is a few years old it will start producing small, yellow flowers in spring. While they are not particularly significant, they are of interest and are followed by small black berries.

Their common name dates back to Victorian times, when palms were first popular as indoor plants. Victorian parlours, filled with fumes from coal fires and gas lamps, were extremely hostile places for plants. That it grew well enough to become a popular plant under these conditions is indicative of just how easy it is to grow. They

soil	Any well-drained, multi-purpose compost. Add crocks to the base of the pot
temp	Provide warm greenhouse conditions, minimum temperature of 10°C (50°F)
water & humidity	Water well from spring to autumn, sparingly in winter. Average humidity. Mist often in high temperatures
general care	Only re-pot when the plant is pot-bound, as it hates disturbance. Top-dress with fresh compost every spring
pests & diseases	Red spider mite and scale insects. Brown tips are usually due to low humidity during warm weather

Chamaedorea elegans

were also particularly popular plants for use in conservatories, and they are still well suited to this environment.

As long as Chamaedorea plants are given a moderate amount of water in summer, and not allowed to dry out too much or to become waterlogged, they should grow well. They particularly resent being waterlogged and stagnant water can lead to the plant developing spotting on the leaves. Add some crocks to the base of pots before you plant them up, to prevent the drainage holes from getting clogged up with compost. They grow best in light shade or filtered light, but will tolerate quite a bit of shade.

Over time the older leaves will start to turn brown and die. This is part of the plants natural process in growth and is not a cause for alarm. Simply use secateurs to remove any brown leaves near the base of the leaf.

Propagation is tricky. They are best grown from seed, but seed needs high temperatures of at least 25°C (77°F) before it will germinate.

There are other species and cultivars available that are just as easy to grow and with slightly different sizes, habits and leaf shapes.

Chamaerops humilis

Dwarf fan palm

If you are looking for a large foliage plant that really makes a statement in the conservatory or greenhouse, Chamaerops is well worth considering. It reaches an impressive size and has a wonderfully dramatic shape. Its numerous leaf stalks explode from the base of the plant and carry huge, fan-shaped leaves.

Chamaerops humilis is a half-hardy plant, and it can be grown outdoors in a container and moved into the greenhouse or conservatory for winter in frost-prone areas. It can even be grown outdoors all year round in areas that only suffer light frosts as it will take a temperature of 0°C (32°F) for a short while. This indicates that it does not need high temperatures. It can be grown in a cool house, but will really thrive if the temperature is a little higher, at at least 10°C (50°F), so if possible grow it in a warm greenhouse. It will benefit from being placed in good, bright, filtered light and given an average humidity. It enjoys fresh air, so take care to ventilate it well, especially in warm spells in summer.

The leaf shape is the most impressive feature of Chamaerops. Thin, glossy leaflets are arranged in a fan around a central point, so forming a great circle of spikes. When the plant is young, these leaves emerge almost from the compost, but as the plant matures, it forms a stem and the new leaves are produced from the top of this. The lower leaves will gradually turn brown and die as the plant grows. This is not a problem and is just a part of the plant's natural habit. Simply cut the dead leaves away as close to the stem as possible.

You will need a fair bit of space to grow this plant. It can grow up to 3m (10ft) in height, but it is unusual for it to grow quite so large in a container. Try to place it in a position where it will not be cramped, so that the leaves are able to grow to their full extent, thereby showing off their dramatic habit.

To propagate from seed, you will need to provide high temperatures and it is often easier to propagate vegetatively, from suckers. These are produced at the side of the main stem. They should be removed in spring. Try to do this at the same time as potting on or top-dressing the plant. Make sure the root ball is wet, and then tip the plant out of its pot before carefully teasing away the suckers. Try to prevent breaking off too much of the sucker's roots and plant it up into fresh compost.

Chamaerops humilis

soil	Any well-drained, multi-purpose compost. Add crocks to the base of the pot
temp	Provide warm greenhouse conditions with a minimum temperature of 10°C (50°F)
water & humidity	Water moderately when actively growing, and sparingly in winter. Average humidity, mist occasionally
general care	Propagation is by seed sown at high temperatures (at least 22°C/72°F) or remove suckers from base
pests & diseases	Red spider mite can occasionally be a problem, but apart from that these plants are fairly trouble free

Chrysanthemum

Growing chrysanthemums for cut flowers is now thought of as a little old-fashioned, although there is no reason why it should be so. Florists' chrysanthemums make excellent use of the shelter of a cold greenhouse.

They make long-lasting cut flowers in a huge number of colours and shapes. They also flower in autumn, when few other homegrown cut flowers are available.

Growing them is a little complicated. The season begins in spring, when rooted cuttings become available. If you have your own plants, take cuttings in late winter. Pot these rooted cuttings up and grow on in the greenhouse. Place these pots outside when danger of frost has passed, and grow them there all summer, watering and feeding well. In early autumn bring them back indoors. Flowers should have started to form.

You will have to decide whether you want sprays or single flowers. Large single flowers are produced by nipping off the side flowers as they form. All of the plant's concentration is then put into the central flower. Sprays of smaller flowers are produced by removing the tip of the stem, so that energy is spread between a number of flowers. Choose 'disbudded' cultivars if you want to grow

soil	Grow in a container in well-drained, compost with extra organic matter added
temp	Provide cold greenhouse conditions and stand outside in summer
water & humidity	Water well when actively growing, particularly when flowers are forming, and keep dry in winter
general care	To get large single blooms you will need to nip out any side blooms as they form. Little else is required
pests & diseases	Aphids, mildew, grey mould, powdery mildew, leaf miner and slugs attack plants. Viruses can be a problem

single flowers, or 'non-disbudded' ones if you want sprays of smaller flowers.

After flowering, the plants should be cut right down to the ground. Let them rest completely for a few weeks before resuming light watering.

Charm and cascade chrysanthemums are sold as pot plants. They are completely covered in small, colourful flowers and there are many different cultivars available. The Charm group usually form dense, rounded mounds, while the Cascade group have trailing stems which can be trained into a colourful waterfall of blooms.

To propagate, tip cuttings taken from early to late winter root easily. As the plants grow, pinch out the tips to encourage a bushy habit. Discard the parent plant.

Chrysanthemum 'Yvonne Arnaud'

	SPRING	SUMMER	AUTUMN	WINTER	height (cm)	spread (cm)	flower colour	
Chrysanthemum 'Dawn Mist'			● ●		120	75		Daisy-like florists' spray chrysanthemum (non-disbudded)
C. 'Hilfred'			● ●		100	100		Charm chrysanthemum with many small flowers
C. 'Primrose John Hughes'			● ●		120	60		Pom-pom shaped florists' chrysanthemum (disbudded)
C. 'Wisley Bronze'			● ●		150	100		Cascade chrysanthemum with yellow flower centres
C. 'Yvonne Arnaud'			● ●		120	75		Dark pink florists' chrysanthemum (disbudded)

● *flowering*

Clerodendrum
Glory bower

The two commonly grown species of clerodendrum are large, exotic climbers with unusual flowers. They require warm conditions to grow well and so need to be grown in warm greenhouse conditions, with a minimum winter temperature of 13°C (55°F).

Clerodendrum thomsoniae

Clerodendrum ugandense

The most widely grown is *Clerodendrum thomsoniae*, more commonly known as the glory bower. It bears large clusters of flowers that look more like inflated white seed pods with small red flowers dangling from them. It flowers in summer. *C. ugandense*, the blue glory bower, bears its flowers in spring and then occasionally through summer and autumn. Its flowers are quite different, being light blue in colour and a far more conventional flower shape than its relative. The flowers have a delicacy and elegance about them, enhanced by their long, fine stamens, which emerge from the top of the flower.

Both plants grow large, to about 3m (10ft) in height. They can be pruned to keep them smaller and this should be carried out as soon as possible after flowering. They can be pruned back hard.

As well as needing high temperatures, they also need high levels of humidity. Misting is unlikely to be particularly effective on such a large plant, so instead make sure that you damp down the area near the plant on a regular basis. Keep the compost moist, but not soggy, at all times throughout the growing season. In winter, both plants will benefit from a period of dormancy, when they should not be watered at all for a few weeks. However, make sure temperatures do not drop below 13°C (55°F) during this resting period.

They will grow best in full sunlight, but need a little shade from midday sun in summer. Provide good ventilation on hot days. Feed once a month with a liquid fertilizer while in growth.

soil	Grow in a large container in well-drained, multi-purpose compost
temp	Grow in warm greenhouse conditions, minimum winter temperature of 13°C (55°F)
water & humidity	Water well from spring to autumn and keep fairly dry in winter. Provide high humidity in hot weather
general care	Plants can be pruned back to keep them down to size immediately after they have finished flowering
pests & diseases	Whiteflies, scale insect, red spider mite and mealy bugs can all attack clerodendrum plants

	SPRING	SUMMER	AUTUMN	WINTER	height (cm)	spread (cm)	flower colour	
Clerodendrum thomsoniae		● ● ●			300	100	▨	Unusual white and red flowers
C. ugandense (C. myricoides 'Ugandense')	●	●			300	100	▨	Delicate blue flowers on large, exotic climber

● flowering

Clianthus
Lobster claw *or*
Parrot's bill

Considering its exotic looks, Clianthus is a fairly easy to grow plant. It does not need a great deal of warmth to thrive and so will grow well in a cool greenhouse, as long as the temperature does not drop below 4°C (39°F).

Clianthus puniceus f. albus

It is actually a shrub, but it is more often treated as a climber. This is because of its long, lax stems. As a shrub the stems are too floppy and the flowers are not shown off to their best, but the plant can easily be trained by tying the stems into a sturdy trellis or a framework of horizontal wires.

Clianthus puniceus has several common names, including parrot's bill and lobster claw, and both describe the shape of it well. The main features of the flowers are the colourful, claw-shaped petals. In *C. puniceus* these are bright red and in *C. puniceus* f. *albus* they are white with an occasional flush of green. They are borne in dense clusters of up to 12 flowers. The foliage of these plants is also attractive. It is soft and delicate, made up of pairs of small leaves arranged along a stem.

These plants can grow fairly large, so make sure that you have enough space before you plant them. They grow best if they are left unpruned, so avoid this if at all possible. Shortening the stems that have flowered is not a problem and may help to contain the plant a little.

A free-draining compost is important, so it is a good idea to incorporate some grit into the compost when first potting up, and to put crocks over the base of the drainage holes to prevent them from clogging up with compost. Water well in summer and feed only occasionally throughout the growing season. Reduce watering in winter but do not allow to dry out completely.

soil	Freely draining, so incorporate extra grit into a multi-purpose compost
temp	Grow in cool greenhouse conditions, minimum 4°C (39°F) in winter
water & humidity	Water well from spring to autumn, while in active growth, sparingly in winter. Requires average humidity
general care	Regularly remove flowers as they fade. Plant resents too much pruning so only carry out if really necessary
pests & diseases	Clianthus is not attacked by many pests or diseases, although it can suffer from red spider mite occasionally

Clianthus puniceus

	SPRING	SUMMER	AUTUMN	WINTER	height (cm)	spread (cm)	flower colour	
Clianthus puniceus	● ● ●				300	200	■	Bears clusters of claw-shaped flowers
C. puniceus f. albus	● ● ●				300	200	□	Clusters of greeny-white flowers

● *flowering*

Clivia miniata

Originating in South Africa, *Clivia miniata* has become an extremely popular plant for conservatories and greenhouses. Thick, strap-shaped, arching leaves grow from the large bulb, and in spring a stout stem appears from these leaves bearing a flower head of exotic, red and orange blooms.

Clivia is generally thought of as tolerant of household conditions as it will take a good deal of shade without suffering. However, this does not necessarily make it an easy plant to grow and flower. In fact, Clivia is a bit of a diva. It simply refuses to perform without a good, long winter rest. This means growing it in a cool greenhouse in which it is possible to lower the temperature to between 4°C (39°F) and 10°C (50°F) for around two months at some point over autumn and winter. It will need to be placed in the coolest spot in the greenhouse during this period to prevent it from getting too hot on occasional warm winter days. Watering must be reduced to almost nothing over this time and feeding should be completely stopped.

After this rest, the plant can be gently coaxed back into life with a little heat and some careful watering. Flower buds will then start to form, but Clivia still has some exacting requirements in order to flower successfully. The temperature over the entire flowering period will need to be kept higher than 16°C (61°F). Do not move or in any way disturb the plant from the time when flower buds start to form until flowering is over, or flowering can abort completely. When grown under these exacting conditions, it should not be too difficult to encourage repeat flowering.

soil	Free draining, so incorporate some extra grit into a multi-purpose compost
temp	Grow in cool greenhouse conditions, minimum 4°C (39°F) temperature in winter
water & humidity	Water freely in summer and sparingly in winter until shoots are a few inches tall. Requires normal humidity
general care	Does not like disturbance. Once buds are forming do not move it. Do not re-pot until absolutely necessary
pests & diseases	Mealy bugs and scale insect cause problems. Too much sun or water can cause yellowing leaves

The dislike of disturbance extends to re-potting too. The roots of clivias are thick and fleshy and hate being disturbed. Because of this, it is advisable to leave the plant in the same pot until it is almost breaking out of it. As well as encouraging flowering, this restricted root run will lead to the formation of small offsets. These can be carefully teased away from the main plant during potting on. They should be potted up in fresh compost and nurtured until they reach flowering size. When you do pot on, do it after the flower spike has died down.

During dividing and re-potting, it is a good idea to wear garden gloves, as Clivia produces an irritating sap. Do not keep the plant where small children can reach it, as it can cause stomach upset if eaten.

Clivia miniata

Cobaea scandens
Cup and saucer vine

Cobaea is a good example of how a greenhouse or conservatory can change the way you look at plants. It is often grown as a colourful, fast-growing annual in temperate areas that are prone to frosts. In a frost-free environment, Cobaea can be grown as a rampant and impressive perennial climber.

Cobaea scandens

Cobaea scandens is grown for its flowers, which emerge a pale, creamy-yellow colour and age to light and then dark purple. It is usual to have many different shades of flowers on the plant at the same time. The common name for cobaea is the cup and saucer vine, and this relates to the shapes of the flowers. The 'cup', actually more bell shaped, sits on a 'saucer' of small green leaf-like structures, known as the calyx.

This is a fairly easy plant to grow from seed, and there is really no need to buy a plant, as it puts on so much growth in its first season. Start seeds off in early spring in a heated propagator. Pot them on into a large pot of multi-purpose compost as soon as they are large enough. You will need to provide some support for them to clamber up. Cobaea plants climb by tendrils and will need little tying in as they are such effective climbers. Provide a trellis or set of horizontal wires for the plant and loosely tie the first few stems to it. The rest of the stems will find their own way. You may find that the plant sends out stray stems that make the plant look messy later in the summer. These can simply be twined round existing growth or tied in loosely.

It is important that Cobaea is planted in a spot where it will receive high levels of light. Lack of light can lead to flowers failing to colour up to their full, deep purple. Plants should be watered well throughout summer and autumn, and then less in winter. Feed once a month throughout summer and autumn. Flowering will continue into autumn, and may even last into winter if temperatures are kept fairly high. From winter to early spring, once flowering has stopped, cut the plant right down to just 5–8cm (2–3in) above the ground and top dress with fresh compost. This will mean that all growth will be fresh for the following year. The plant flowers on new growth and puts on a lot of growth in one season, so there is really little point in keeping any of the old stems.

soil	Cobaea will grow well in a container in any multi-purpose compost
temp	Grow in cool greenhouse conditions, a minimum 4°C (39°F) in winter
water & humidity	Water well in summer when the plant is in active growth and less in winter. Requires average humidity
general care	Seed will germinate easily with some heat in spring and seedlings will quickly grow into large plants
pests & diseases	If plant allowed to dry out in summer aphids can attack growing tips. Red spider mite can also be a problem

Crinodendron hookerianum

Crinodendron is often seen growing in gardens in temperate areas. The plant is frost hardy and will survive outside. It is grown as a greenhouse plant because of the damage done to the young foliage and flower buds by frost.

Crinodendron hookerianum

trouble over. Crinodendron is an evergreen plant and its leaves are handsome, dark green and glossy. The flowers are beautiful. They hang down from the branches in small groups. Each grows on the end of a slightly arched stem, and is thick and waxy and shaped like a tiny lantern. The colour is a deep, raspberry pink.

They like to be planted in a slightly acidic soil and so are good plants to grow in pots, where ericaceous compost can be used. Mix this with a little leaf mould or other organic matter. In order to keep the soil acidic, water with soft water. If you live in a hard-water area, you will need to collect fresh rainwater, and use it on the plant as soon as possible. They should be placed in partial shade and will appreciate good ventilation in summer, particularly on hot days.

They grow into large plants, so you will need to provide a particularly big pot to keep them happy. Size can become a bit of a problem, as they should not really be extensively pruned. However, you can carry out a little pruning each year, which will help to prevent them from taking up too much space. Trim back all of the shoots lightly and then remove any stems that are crossing the centre of the plant, making it congested, or that have died back or are damaged. The best time to carry this out is immediately after the flowers have faded, as this will prevent you from cutting off any ripening wood or flower buds.

Crinodendron plants are extremely unlikely to be actually killed by a frost. However, even though the damage caused is superficial, it can ruin the look of the plant, and ultimately prevent it from being worth garden space. The young foliage and flower buds are blackened and marked by frost. This is not an occasional event, but can occur year after year in areas that suffer regular frosts. In many areas, enjoying an unmarked display of flowers and foliage will be the exception to the norm. By growing the plant in a greenhouse that is kept just frost-free, the foliage and flowers will be left unmarked.

They are well worth taking the

soil	Grows best in a container in ericaceous compost with added organic matter
temp	Frost hardy, but grow in cool greenhouse conditions, minimum 4°C (39°F)
water & humidity	Water well in summer when the plant is in active growth and less in winter. Requires average humidity
general care	Best if not pruned too extensively. Lightly prune after flowering in finished in late summer or autumn
pests & diseases	Crinodendron plants do not suffer from major problems with any particular pests and diseases

Cupressus torulosa 'Cashmiriana'

Kashmir cypress

Few plants have the poise and elegance of *Cupressus torulosa* 'Cashmeriana'. Although columnar when young, it is a beautiful foliage plant that has weeping branches from which hang curtains of finely divided blue-green leaves.

Cupressus torulosa 'Cashmeriana'

It is unusual to grow a conifer under glass, as most of them are from cold regions of the world and so extremely hardy. They also grow very large. *C. t.* 'Cashmeriana' is a good exception to this rule that is worth making space for in either the greenhouse or conservatory. It not hardy enough to tolerate the frosts of an average temperate winter. It also hates being kept too wet, and needs the shelter of a glasshouse to keep winter wet away from its roots. It can be kept compact.

It is a good plant for providing a fine foil of leaves behind other foliage plants, but it is attractive enough to act as a specimen plant in its own right. For this it will need space. In the wild it can grow up to 30m (100ft) in height and up to 10m (33ft) across, but it can be kept much smaller if grown in a container in a glasshouse or conservatory. It will generally not grow any taller than 2m (6½ft) under these conditions, depending on the size of the container. It is not suitable for planting out into a border, as it will then grow far too large for the average greenhouse or conservatory. These plants can be pruned to help keep them down to size, but only lightly, and you will have to be extremely careful not to lose the plant's graceful outline. Hard pruning is not possible without ruining the shape of the plant so should be avoided.

It is a good idea to pot Cupressus up regularly, every year or so, but do so into only slightly larger pots each time, to restrict growth. Top dress with fresh compost in the years when the plant is not potted on. Cupressus plants should be placed in a spot where they will get full light. They appreciate being watered well in summer, but will also tolerate fairly dry conditions – another reason why they are suitable for container culture. It is particularly important not to over water them in winter, as this can lead to roots rotting. Feed plants once a month with a liquid feed throughout the growing season. In warm weather in summer they will appreciate good ventilation to help cool them down.

soil	Grow best in a container in a tree and shrub compost with good drainage
temp	Grow in warm greenhouse conditions with a minimum temperature of 7°C (45°F)
water & humidity	Water well in summer when the plant is in active growth and less in winter. Requires average humidity
general care	Not suitable for hard pruning, but can be lightly pruned each year in spring if necessary
pests & diseases	Scale insect and aphids can attack. Plants may suffer from root rot if kept too wet and cold

Cycas revoluta

Cycad *or* Japanese sago palm

Cycads have bizarre and exotic looks. These slow-growing, palm-shaped plants produce tough, arching leaf stalks, covered in spiny leaflets. As new leaves are produced, the old ones die away forming a solid, chunky trunk.

Cycads are primitive plants, dominating the earth's flora over 200 million years ago. However, they are now in decline in the wild and only grow in small areas of Asia.

They were popular as houseplants in Victorian times, but have only become popular again in the last few years. *Cycas revoluta* is commonly known as the Japanese sago palm. It makes a good specimen plant for the greenhouse or conservatory as it has such a striking shape and it is not too tricky to look after. Because of its primitive looks, it suits being grouped together with ferns, another ancient plant group. However, take care when doing this as cycads do not need nearly the same amount of watering or the same levels of humidity that most ferns require.

Cycads will tolerate a good deal of light, although keep them away from the hottest midday sun. Water them only moderately in summer and even less in winter. Mist occasionally, cutting back on both in

soil	Will grow best in compost that has been mixed with bark chippings and grit
temp	Grow in warm greenhouse with minimum temperature of 7°C (45°F)
water & humidity	Water carefully in summer and provide average humidity. Reduce humidity and watering in winter
general care	To propagate, remove suckers from around the base of the plant when re-potting in spring
pests & diseases	Red spider mite, scale insect and mealy bugs can all cause problems, but otherwise trouble free

winter. Try to use soft water if possible. If you live in a hard-water area, this will mean collecting fresh rainwater. Collect small amounts of rainwater regularly, rather than using a large water butt, as pests and diseases can be harboured in water that is left to stand for a while. If you live in a soft-water area, use the tap water, but allow it to stand until it is tepid before watering the plant. Occasionally you will need to remove the dead leaves by cutting them back to the point at which they grow from the trunk.

Plants grow slowly and so you should expect to pay a high price for a large plant. The upside of this is that the plants live for many years, and in fact are likely to outlive their owners by a long time. If you manage to keep it growing well over many years you will have an extremely valuable plant.

It is worth noting that the individual leaflets can be tough and spiky, and they may not be good plants to have around young children for this reason. They are intolerant of chemical pesticides, so if you do have an infestation of pests, try to deal with it by manually removing them or by using a soft soap spray.

Cycas revoluta close up

Cycas revoluta

Cyclamen

The cyclamen mentioned here are extremely suitable for growing in greenhouses and conservatories. Cultivars of _Cyclamen persicum_ appear in shops in late autumn and remain available until late winter.

Cyclamen persicum

soil	Will grow best in compost that has been mixed with bark chippings and grit
temp	Warm greenhouse, minimum 7°C (41°F); some tolerate cooler temperature
water & humidity	Water carefully in summer and provide average humidity. Reduce humidity and watering in winter
general care	To propagate, remove suckers from around the base of the plant when re-potting in spring
pests & diseases	Red spider mite, scale insect and mealy bugs can all cause problems, otherwise trouble free

Flowers are available in white, pink and purple, and all shades in between; some are even sweetly scented. They need warm greenhouse conditions or can be flowered in the home and then moved out into a cool greenhouse to rest. _C. africanum_ and _C. libanoticum_ are both half hardy and so need far cooler conditions. They are suitable for growing in a cool greenhouse.

Given the right conditions, a single plant of _C. persicum_ will flower for several months. In winter, when the plant is flowering and in leaf, it is important to mist the leaves occasionally and to keep the compost moist. Take care not to wet the crowns when watering or they can suffer from rots. Watering straight into the tray will allow the roots to take up water but will prevent water splashing on crowns.

Cyclamen plants are often thrown away after flowering has finished. This is a shame as they are easy to keep alive and to encourage to flower again. After flowering, the foliage will start to die down. Reduce watering at this time. Once danger of frost has passed, place the plant, in its pot, into a cold frame or cool greenhouse. Laying it on its side will prevent moisture getting into the crown. The crowns will remain dormant for a few months, during which time they need to be kept completely dry. In late summer, plants can be brought back into a cool room in the house. They should then be top dressed, watered and fed to encourage the formation of flower buds.

Cyclamen appreciate being pot bound, so wait until tubers completely fill the pot before splitting and re-potting. This should be carried out while the plant is dormant.

	SPRING	SUMMER	AUTUMN	WINTER	height (cm)	spread (cm)	flower colour	
Cyclamen africanum			● ● ●		15	23		Half hardy plant with delicate pink flowers
C. libanoticum	●			● ● ●	10	15		Half-hardy winter-flowering plant
C. persicum	●			● ● ●	20	15		Warm greenhouse or house plant, many cultivars available

● *flowering*

Cymbidium

The flowers of Cymbidium are borne in a tall, usually arching, flower spike. They often densely cover the spike to form a thick tower of flowers. They make spectacular flowering plants for conservatories and greenhouses.

Each individual flower comprises five petals and a central lip, often in a contrasting colour. Hundred of good cultivars are available in colours including yellow, pink, red, green and white. The flower spikes, once formed, are long lasting.

To flower at their best, cymbidiums need many hours of daylight, so place them in the sunniest spot you have available. Shade them only from the hottest midday summer sun and keep them well ventilated. Do not provide any shade at all throughout winter as they will then need the maximum light available. In low light, flowers may fail to form and the plant will look lacklustre and may even start to wilt and droop. *Cymbidium eburneum* is among the easiest of these to grow and flower, so is a good plant to start with if you have not grown them before.

Cymbidiums should be fed occasionally over summer with a half-strength liquid feed. They should be watered moderately in summer and even less in winter. Keep the humidity high by misting plants at least once a day and place trays of damp peat or moist expanded clay granules under the pot or near the plant. Place plants near other humidity lovers, such as ferns, and damp the whole area down regularly, particularly in hot weather. Do not re-pot until absolutely necessary, as Cymbidiums dislike disturbance. The roots should be almost breaking out of the pot before they are potted on. Take the opportunity to propagate when you do pot it on. Do this by dividing the root ball in half or into smaller pieces, depending on the size of the plant. Pot up each section into fresh orchid compost.

soil	Grow Cymbidiums in an open orchid compost, containing bark and charcoal
temp	Grow in a warm greenhouse that is kept at a minimum temperature of 10°C (50°F)
water & humidity	Water carefully in summer and less in winter. Use soft water only. Provide high levels of humidity
general care	Divide plants in spring and pot each section into fresh compost. Only divide pot-bound plants
pests & diseases	In low humidity, red spider mite can be a problem. Other likely pests include aphids and mealy bugs

Cymbidium 'Showgirl'

	SPRING	SUMMER	AUTUMN	WINTER	height (cm)	spread (cm)	flower colour	
Cymbidium eburneum				● ● ●	50	60		Large flower spikes and pale flowers
C. 'Showgirl'				● ● ●	45	30		Produces densely covered flower spikes

● *flowering*

Cyperus involucratus (syn. C. alternifolius)

Umbrella plant

Cyperus involucratus is known as the umbrella plant because of its long leaf stalk topped with a circle of slender, shiny green leaves. The species suitable for growing in greenhouses and conservatories are related to the papyrus plant, which was used by the ancient Egyptians to make paper.

Cyperus involucratus

If properly looked after, Cyperus species make tall and elegant foliage plants. Their greatest requirement is for moisture, and the key to keeping them looking good is to give them lots of water and high humidity. They should really never be allowed to dry out and should be stood in a tray of water at all times. This keeps the roots moist and also helps to raise the humidity around the leaves of the plant.

In addition to this, you should regularly mist the foliage, otherwise the ends of the leaves are likely to dry out and turn brown. You can also stand a tray of moist pebbles or expanded clay granules nearby, as the water from these evaporates slowly and keeps the humidity high. Placing the plant in an area with other humidity-loving plants will also help, as you can then regularly damp down the paths and benches around them, further increasing the humidity.

During summer, provide some shade or place the plant under a larger plant so that it is in dappled shade. In winter, however, the plant will appreciate being placed in a spot that receives good light all day long.

C. involucratus bears its circle of leaves at the top of tall slender stems that can grow up to 90cm (3ft) in height. Plants grow quickly and they should be potted on every year in order to avoid checking their growth. Some old stems will eventually die away. Do not panic if this happens as it is part of the plant's natural growth process. Once the dead stems are removed young, fresh shoots will appear that will eventually grow even larger than those they have replaced.

Small yellow flowers sometimes appear on the tops of the leaf stalks above the leaves in summer. Although pretty, they are fairly inconsequential and the plant is really grown for the overall impact of its foliage.

Cyperus plants are easily propagated by dividing them when carrying out re-potting in spring. Pot each section up into fresh compost and take care to keep the compost wet while the new plant is getting established.

soil	Will be happy situated in a good, multi-purpose compost
temp	Grow in a cool greenhouse that is kept at a minimum temperature of 5°C (41°F)
water & humidity	Keep constantly moist by standing container in a tray of water. Reduce watering in winter. High humidity
general care	Old stems will eventually turn brown and die. They should be cut off at the base of the plant
pests & diseases	Aphids can occur if the atmosphere is too dry. Brown tips to leaves caused by dry air or compost

Desfontainea spinosa

Desfontainea is among a group of conservatory plants that are almost completely hardy. It is often grown out of doors in temperate regions, particularly in warmer or coastal areas. However, in any slightly harsher conditions, it is not hardy, and this is why it is sometimes grown as a conservatory or frost-free greenhouse plant.

It is a compact, attractive shrub that could be grown for its leaves alone. These are glossy and deep green in colour. They are shaped like miniature holly leaves and are evergreen, making this an attractive and useful plant all year round. However, from mid-summer right through until the end of autumn it produces an impressive and long-running display of bright red flowers that are tipped with yellow. These are tubular in shape and dangle gracefully from the branches.

The problem with growing *Desfontainea spinosa* out of doors really comes down to wind – they cannot tolerate the drying effects of a cold wind. In a conservatory or greenhouse this is obviously not an issue. It is not necessary therefore to provide high temperatures for them, and they may even grow well in an unheated greenhouse as this environment will provide all the shelter from wind that the plant needs. However, for best results grow desfontainea in a greenhouse that is kept just frost-free.

It is important that plants are sited in a peaty compost and it is essential that any compost they are grown in is lime-free. An ericaceous compost is the best choice. They will really grow well if given a good, deep pot to get their roots down into.

soil	Will be happy to grow in a good multi-purpose compost
temp	Grow in a cool greenhouse that is kept at a minimum temperature of 5°C (41°F)
water & humidity	Keep soil moist by standing container in tray of water. Reduce watering slightly in winter. High humidity
general care	Old stems will eventually turn brown and die. They should be cut off at the base of the plant
pests & diseases	Aphids can occur if atmosphere too dry. Brown tips to leaves caused by dry air or compost

The soil should be kept moist at all times, even in winter, although it should be kept a little dryer in winter than during the summer.

Water with soft water to prevent the soil's pH from changing. If you live in a hard-water area, this will entail collecting fresh rainwater and using it as soon as possible to water the plant. Avoid using water from a water butt or indeed any water that has been left to sit for a long time, as this may have been colonized by pests or diseases.

Place plants in a position where they will receive dappled or partial shade. Underneath the shade of other plants is perfect. Although desfontainea eventually grows large, up to 2m (6½ft) in height and spread, it does this slowly and will make a neat and compact plant for the conservatory or greenhouse for several years. When it is not in flower, use its deep green, glossy leaves as a foil for other flowers.

Desfontainea spinosa

Dianthus
Carnation

Dianthus plants are better known as carnations. Some are grown as border plants out of doors, but those suited to growing in the conservatory and greenhouse are usually grown as cut flowers.

It may seem slightly old fashioned to use your greenhouse space to grow cut flowers, particularly carnations, but it is immensely satisfying. These plants make good cut flowers that can last for weeks and bring colour and even scent into the home. Dianthus make particularly good cut flowers, as they produce their blooms all year round. The two types to look out for are Malmaison carnations and perpetual-flowering carnations. Both are suitable for cut-flower production and enjoy the conditions in a cool greenhouse.

soil	Will grow best if planted into a good multi-purpose compost
temp	Grow in a cool greenhouse that is kept at a minimum temperature of 7°C (45°F)
water & humidity	Water well in spring and summer, sparingly in autumn and winter. Low humidity, particularly in winter
general care	Replace old plants by taking cuttings in late winter. Provide stable and constant temperatures
pests & diseases	Aphids, red spider mite and thrips can all attack and cause problems for Dianthus plants

Dianthus 'Rifif'

They are often started off as cuttings in winter. They should be cut back once they have rooted so that they are just a few inches tall. Keep them fairly dry throughout winter and start watering and feeding in early spring. It is important to provide them with a good, even temperature and regular but not excessive watering if you want to produce the best flowers. Flowers can form at any time of year. They are generally too tall to support themselves and they may flop over if not given adequate support. Push a bamboo cane or similar into the soil next to the plant when a flower starts to form. As the flower stem grows, tie it in at intervals. It is common practice to remove any flower buds that appear on the sides of the flower stem as it grows. This will allow the plant to put all of its energy into producing one large bloom at the top of the stem. Cut the stem when the flower has started to colour up. Cut it between the nodes and place it in water.

In autumn, allow the plant to dry out a little, and keep it fairly dry until the following spring.

	SPRING	SUMMER	AUTUMN	WINTER	height (cm)	spread (cm)	flower colour
Dianthus 'Duchess of Westminster'	● ● ●	● ● ●	● ● ●	● ● ●	60	40	Single coloured flowers in lovely pale pink
D. 'Nina'	● ● ●	● ● ●	● ● ●	● ● ●	130	30	Single coloured dark red flowers
D. 'Rifif'	● ● ●	● ● ●	● ● ●	● ● ●	130	30	Attractive picotee edging to flowers
D. 'Souvenir de la Malmaison'	● ● ●	● ● ●	● ● ●	● ● ●	60	40	Malmaison carnation with pink flowers
D. 'White Sim'	● ● ●	● ● ●	● ● ●	● ● ●	130	30	Perpetual-flowering carnation

● *flowering*

Epiphyllum

Epiphyllum plants are large succulents with beautiful big flowers. Some of the species have flowers that open only at night and some that open only during the day. Many Epiphyllums are scented.

Epiphyllum crenatum can reach up to 3m (10ft) in height and spread. It has creamy-white flowers encased in pink outer petals. *E. anguliger* is much more compact, reaching less than 1m (3ft) in height. It has yellow flowers.

Unlike other cacti, Epiphyllum plants are happy in a standard compost. They originally come from forest environments and will appreciate a little peat mixed into the compost. Again unusually for cacti, they sometimes appreciate a fairly high humidity, particularly if the weather is warm.

soil	Best grown if planted into a good multi-purpose compost with a little added peat
temp	Grow in warm greenhouse conditions with a minimum temperature of 10°C (50°F)
water & humidity	Water fairly well in summer, and sparingly in winter, keeping compost just moist. High humidity in hot weather
general care	Must have a period of rest after flowering, with cool temperatures and almost no water
pests & diseases	Mealy bugs and aphids can attack and cause problems for Epiphyllum plants, but there is little else

Epiphyllum crenatum

All Epiphyllums need special treatment in order to flower reliably each year. Water well while the plant is in flower but after flowering give it a period of rest. This should be in a lower temperature than previously and the plant should be given less water than it has been having. After a few weeks you can begin normal watering again. New growth will appear. Keep the plant dry and cool over winter. Give a small amount of water every month or so over this time to prevent the compost from completely drying out. In late spring small flower buds should start to form on the plant. At this time, start to gradually increase watering and temperature, but do not move the plant after buds have appeared or they may drop. The plant should start flowering in early summer.

It is important to follow this regime as Epiphyllum plants will suffer if given too much or too little water at the wrong time of year, just as they can suffer if the temperature is too warm or too cool. Their stems can shrivel and brown spots can appear on them.

	SPRING	SUMMER	AUTUMN	WINTER	height (cm)	spread (cm)	flower colour	
Epiphyllum anguliger		● ● ● ●			75	45		Large yellow and white flowers
E. crenatum		● ● ●			300	300		Flowers close at night

● *flowering*

79

Fatsia japonica

Fatsia is grown for its huge, glossy, palm-shaped leaves. It is an easy plant to grow and, as long as it is given some fairly basic care, it will grow into an impressive specimen plant quickly and with little fuss.

It is often seen growing outside in temperate areas as it is fairly hardy. However, its large, glossy leaves tend to get a little tattered and the worse for wear over the average winter, and the plant does not look nearly as impressive as it does when grown in the shelter of a conservatory or greenhouse.

While *Fatsia japonica* plants will tolerate a fair amount of shade, there are variegated cultivars that need fairly bright light or their colours will fade. It really needs to be shaded from hot summer sun, as this can scorch and shrivel the leaves. In hot summer weather try to provide good ventilation or to move the plant out of doors into a shady spot.

They are, however, generally unfussy plants, and their only definite requirement is for a cool temperature in winter – they can be moved out to a cool greenhouse if the conservatory is too warm over this time. Watering and feeding are all fairly standard, and they will appreciate being misted occasionally to raise the humidity, particularly when the temperature is high in summer. Another way of raising the humidity is to sponge their leaves down occasionally. This also keeps them looking clean and glossy. Alternatively, group them with other humidity lovers such as ferns, and regularly damp down the paths and benches nearby.

In the wild, Fatsia plants can grow large, but in containers in a conservatory or greenhouse they should stay at a manageable size. As they grow so quickly. buy a small one and pot on every year and you will soon have a specimen plant. To prevent it from getting leggy, cut back the growing tips

before new growth emerges each spring. This will help to keep a good bushy shape. If your Fatsia does get too large or leggy, you can cut back really hard without damaging it. Cut back so that just a few leaves remain, and fresh new leaves will soon appear.

In autumn, fatsias often produce large white flower heads. You can enjoy these before cutting them off, but removing them before flowering occurs will help to keep the foliage in the best condition.

soil	Will thrive if planted into a good multi-purpose compost
temp	Grow in cool greenhouse conditions with a minimum temperature of 4°C (39°F)
water & humidity	Water normally during summer, sparingly in winter. High humidity, particularly during warm weather
general care	If the plant grows too large for its space or grows leggy, it will regenerate well from being cut back hard
pests & diseases	Mealy bugs and scale insects can occur. Leaves become brown, spotted or pale if under watered

Fatsia japonica

Ficus
Fig

Plants in the genus Ficus are commonly known as figs. They are a group of plants that cover just about every habit and leaf type. Some have large glossy leaves and an upright habit, while others have tiny leaves and creep across the ground.

Ficus pumila

Ficus benjamina

Figs need warm conditions and so may be better suited to a warm conservatory than to a greenhouse, unless you can provide hothouse conditions.

The best known are the cultivars of *Ficus elastica*, commonly known as the rubber plant or India rubber tree. They have one central stem from which appear large, almost oval, glossy leaves. These plants can grow extremely large and may need to be pruned in winter to keep their size down. They also often lose their lower leaves as they age, giving the plant a leggy look. Similar in habit is the fiddle-leaf fig, *F. lyrata*. Its leaves are broader at the tips than at the bases. They are solid, glossy and dark green in colour.

F. benjamina, commonly known as the weeping fig, has fine branches that divide many times, giving the plant a delicate, tree-like shape. It is covered in small oval leaves. A popular cultivar is *F. benjamina* 'Variegata', which has green leaves edged in cream. A particular problem suffered by the weeping figs is that of suddenly dropping their leaves. This usually happens as a result of being moved, or if the plant has been left in a draught or in low light conditions. Ensure an even temperature at all times and a draught-free position.

F. pumila is a creeping type. It can be grown in a number of different ways. Given a support it can climb well but it looks just as good when grown as a trailing plant. In the wild these plants are creepers and grow gradually along the ground, putting down roots as they go. It has a need for particularly high humidity and should be misted daily in summer.

Ficus benjamina 'Variegata'

soil	Grows best planted into a good multi-purpose compost with a little added peat
temp	Grow in hot house situation (minimum 15°C/59°F) or in a warm conservatory
water & humidity	Water normally during summer, sparingly in winter using tepid water. Creeping types need high humidity
general care	Undertake any pruning in winter. If carried out in spring the plant loses lots of sap
pests & diseases	Red spider mite, scale insects, thrips and mealy bugs can occur. Dry air or over watering leads to leaf drop

	SPRING	SUMMER	AUTUMN	WINTER	height (cm)	spread (cm)	leaf colour	
Ficus benjamina	✹✹✹	✹✹✹	✹✹✹	✹✹✹	200	100		Large plant with elegant foliage
F. benjamina 'Variegata'	✹✹✹	✹✹✹	✹✹✹	✹✹✹	200	100		Variegated colouring to foliage
F. elastica	✹✹✹	✹✹✹	✹✹✹	✹✹✹	400	100		The classic India rubber plant
F. lyrata	✹✹✹	✹✹✹	✹✹✹	✹✹✹	200	100		Fiddle-shaped leaves
F. pumila	✹✹✹	✹✹✹	✹✹✹	✹✹✹	100	50		Tiny-leaved climber or trailer

✹ flowering

Freesia

Freesias are sought after cut flowers, combining a wide range of colours and a lovely shaped flower with a distinctive and delicious scent. They are easy to grow from corms in a conservatory or greenhouse. They need fairly cool temperatures.

Choose plants for good scent – those in pale colours are said to be the most fragrant. Yellow-flowered *Freesia* 'Aurora' is grown for its scent. There are both double- and single-flowered forms. A good double is the pure white *F.* 'Diana'.

Freesia corms can be bought in garden centres and should be planted up in late summer or early autumn. They need good drainage, so plant them into a multi-purpose compost that has had some grit incorporated into it. You should also place crocks over the planting holes, to prevent them from becoming blocked up with compost. Plant corms about an inch deep in the soil and cover over. Once they are planted you should water them carefully as they start into life. During this time they will

soil	Will grow well if planted into a well-drained, multi-purpose compost. Add grit
temp	Cool house conditions where temperatures do not rise above 16°C (61°F)
water & humidity	Water well except after flowering; water should then be reduced until compost is dry and plant dormant
general care	Store the dried corms in a cool, frost-free place and plant them out into fresh compost in late summer
pests & diseases	Red spider mites and aphids can be a problem, particularly if plants are kept in too warm a temperature

Freesia 'Striped Jewel'

need fairly cool temperatures, so take care to provide good ventilation and some dappled shade. They can be placed, in their pots, out of doors over this time in a shady and sheltered spot. Bring them indoors in autumn, before frosts. They will flower in late winter or early spring.

Flowers open in a one-sided spray, and the bottom flower opens first. Pick the flowers when the bottom flower is almost completely open and some of the other buds have started to colour up. They should last for at least one week if kept in water in fairly low temperatures.

After flowering, start feeding the plants, and gradually reduce watering so that the foliage dies down. Once this has happened, dig up the corms and store them in a dark, dry place until the following summer, when they should be planted up in fresh compost.

	SPRING	SUMMER	AUTUMN	WINTER	height (cm)	spread (cm)	flower colour	
Freesia 'Aurora'	●	✎	✎	●	45	20	▫	Scented flowers. Colour darkens towards petal edges
F. 'Diana'	●	✎	✎	●	45	20	▫	Double, white flowers
F. 'Striped Jewel'	●	✎	✎	●	40	20	▪	White throats to purple flowers in striped flecks

✎ planting   ● flowering

Fuchsia

Fuchsia suffers from a bit of an image problem, as most people only know the fussy, fully double kinds in sugary shades of pink and white. This is most probably because these fuchsias make fantastic greenhouse and conservatory plants.

However, there is much more to the genus than this, and there are a number of plants that have a real elegance and sophistication.

Many people love the overblown frilly types, and with good reason. They create impressive displays of flowers and will bloom for months on end, continuing into winter if given the correct conditions. For a slightly toned down version of those fat, dumpling-shaped flowers, opt for a plant such as

F. 'Annabel' with almost pure white flowers or *F.* 'Lady Thumb' in dark pink and white. However, if you are looking for something a little more unusual you could try *F. boliviana* var. *alba*, which bears dense bunches of slender white flowers with red star-shaped flowers at the ends, or *F. fulgens*, which bears slender dark salmon-pink flowers. Both of these plants grows far too large for the average conservatory but, like all fuchsias, they can be cut down almost to the ground every spring if necessary to keep them down to size. As fuchsias flower on new growth, this will make no difference to their displays. *F.* 'Thalia' is a smaller plant with unusual looks. It has dark-green foliage with a purple underside that beautifully sets off its slender dark orange flowers.

soil	Fuchsias grow well if planted into any good multi-purpose compost
temp	Grow in cool house where temperatures do not drop below 5°C (41°F)
water & humidity	Water well during growing season, less in autumn and leave almost dry in winter. High humidity
general care	Cut back hard in early spring if necessary to keep down to size as flowers are borne on new growth
pests & diseases	Red spider mites, vine weevil, grey mould, whitefly and aphids can all be a problem on fuchsias

Even if you are not going to cut the plant back fully in spring, it is a good idea to give it a bit of a prune, as this will help it to remain dense and bushy. Pinch out the growing tips in spring to encourage lots of branching growth. Feed plants every now and then with a liquid feed throughout the growing season.

	SPRING	SUMMER	AUTUMN	WINTER	height (cm)	spread (cm)	flower colour	
Fuchsia 'Annabel'		●●●	●●●		40	40		White, double flowers with hints of pink
F. boliviana var. alba		●●●	●●●		150	100		Long, thin, delicate flowers
F. fulgens		●●●	●●●		100	70		Slender and elegant salmon pink flowers
F. 'Lady Thumb'		●●●	●●●		30	30		Almost hardy shrub with double flowers
F. 'Thalia'		●●●	●●●		60	60		Dark foliage sets off slender orange flowers

● flowering

Gardenia jasminoides

The graceful, old-fashioned good looks and the delicious smell of Gardenia make it a long-standing favourite among conservatory plants. It seems to have everything. The flowers are produced in subtle shades of cream, white and yellow, yet have showy, double petals and an intoxicating scent.

The leaves are dark green and extremely glossy, and make gardenia an attractive plant even when it is not flowering.

Unfortunately, however, gardenia is not necessarily an easy indoor plant. While it is fairly easy simply to keep alive, the eagerly anticipated flower buds have a tendency to drop off unceremoniously if conditions are not absolutely perfect. They will need a year-round source of indirect light and an even temperature to open fully. Ensuring that the plant does not dry out but is also not allowed to get waterlogged during the growing season will also contribute to a good show of flowers.

soil	This plant will grow well if planted into a good ericaceous compost
temp	Grow in hot house at a minimum of 16°C (61°F) or in a warm conservatory
water & humidity	Water well using soft, tepid water during growing season and less in winter. High humidity all year round
general care	Needs even temperature and good light throughout the year to prevent flower buds dropping before they open
pests & diseases	Whiteflies, stem and root mealy bugs and botrytis. Watering with hard water causes leaves to turn yellow

Getting a crop of flowers during the plant's second year can be tricky. You will need to ensure good even, nighttime temperatures of between 16°C (61°F) and 18°C (64°F) and try to keep the daytime temperature at between 21°C (70°F) and 23°C (73°F) while buds are forming in spring. This makes it a plant only for the hot house or for a warm conservatory that is kept heated at night.

Plants grown in hard water areas can suffer and they will show distress by their glossy, dark leaves turning yellow. To avoid this, try to water with soft water as often as possible. Collect fresh rainwater in a bowl and use immediately or as soon as you have collected enough. Gardenias can also suffer from being watered with cold water. When using tap water, draw off a watering can full and leave it sitting for a few hours until it is at room temperature. They will need to be grown in a lime-free, ericaceous compost and the same must be used when re-potting the plant every few years.

Gardenias in the wild are fairly large plants, and if they live for several years they can reach a height of up to 1.8m (6ft). However, it is easy to keep them at a more manageable size. They will need pruning once a year to remain in good shape. The best time to do this is in late winter, just before the new growth starts. Prune back to about four leaf joints above the base of the plant and cut just above where the leaf joins the stem.

Gardenia jasminoides

Gerbera

Gerbera are bold and pretty daisy-shaped flowers that are popular as cut flowers. They do not have the old-fashioned image of many of the other plants that are grown as cut flowers in conservatories and greenhouses.

Gerberas are bright and attractive, and are often seen in modern floral arrangements.

They do not have to be grown as cut flowers, and also make lovely pot plants. They form a neat rosette of bright green leaves from which their succulent stems arise. If you are growing as a pot plant, choose a more compact cultivar rather than the species, *Gerbera jamesonii*. A group of plants known as the Pandora Series, reaching just 25cm (10in) in height, make good candidates for a pot. Unusually for gerberas, which are most often found in bold, bright colours, the flowers of the Pandora Series are in attractive pastel shades.

Gerberas like a good amount of moisture in summer, and should even be kept slightly moist in winter, although you should take care not to over water. They should be fed once a month over the growing season. Place them in a spot where they will receive good light, but shade them from the heat of the midday summer sun. Re-pot every year in fresh compost in spring.

soil	Will grow well if planted into a good multi-purpose compost
temp	Grow in cool greenhouse conditions with a minimum temperature of 5°C (41°F)
water & humidity	Water well during growing season and less in winter, but keep compost moist. Needs normal humidity
general care	Pot into fresh compost in a slightly larger pot every year in spring, just as the new growth is beginning
pests & diseases	Aphids and whiteflies can be a problem, particularly on young growth. Over watering can lead to root rot

If you are growing these plants as cut flowers, you will need to care for the flowers in a particular way to stop them from collapsing. If the stems are not turgid, the stem will quickly collapse. Water the plant well the night before you cut the flower. Once you have cut flowers, drop them into a deep bucket of water so that the stems are completely submerged, leaving only the flower out of the water. Leave them like this for a couple of hours and they will last far longer than if they had not received this treatment.

Gerbera jamesonii

	SPRING	SUMMER	AUTUMN	WINTER	height (cm)	spread (cm)	flower colour	
Gerbera jamesonii		● ● ●			45	60		Large orange daisy flowers
G. Pandora Series		● ● ●			25	40		Bear many flowers on each plant
G. Sunburst Series		● ● ● ●			45	60		Large flowers in bright colours

● *flowering*

Gloriosa superba 'Citrina'

Glory lily

The glory lily, *Gloriosa superba* 'Citrina', is a wonderfully exotic and surprisingly easy plant to grow in a conservatory or greenhouse. It grows from tubers, which should be planted and dug up each year.

Gloriosa superba 'Citrina'

Once you have mastered digging up and replanting the tubers, you will find few problems in producing an impressive display of flowers year after year.

Gloriosa is a climbing plant. Its tubers, planted in spring, send out long growths with tendrils on the ends for climbing up supports. You will need to provide some kind of a framework for the plant to climb up, although it need not be particularly sturdy, as Gloriosa is fairly delicate in its growth habit. The plants can grow up to 2m (6½ft) in height, but are unlikely to get uncontrollable, as the foliage dies down each winter. It is important to provide good drainage, so try mixing some grit into a multi-purpose compost and make sure you put some crocks in the base of the pot to prevent the drainage holes from becoming blocked with compost.

You will be able to buy tubers from garden centres in spring. Choose the largest tubers you can find. It is possible to grow plants from seed, but young plants can take a few years to flower and so it is usually best to start off with the tubers. Plant them 5–8cm (2–3in) deep and water carefully. It is extremely easy to over water plants at this stage, so keep the soil just slightly moist. As shoots start to appear, increase watering gradually. When the plant is in full growth you can water it freely and apply a liquid feed once a month.

Flowers will start to appear in early summer and will be produced right through until the autumn. The flowers look very similar to lily flowers with extremely reflexed petals, and the stamens curl back towards the petals, adding to the windswept effect. The petals are bright yellow in colour and are tinted or striped with deep purple-red. They have slightly wavy edges, giving them a flame-like appearance.

Towards late autumn, start cutting back on watering and stop feeding. Gradually the plant will die back to its tuber, and you should decrease watering in line with the level of dormancy the plant has reached. Once all of the growth has completely died down, remove it and dig up the tubers. Store them in a dry, warm place until it is time to replant them the following spring.

To propagate Gloriosa, split the tubers in spring and re-pot them separately before growing them on as normal.

Gloriosa superba 'Citrina'

soil	Requires a well-drained, multi-purpose compost. Add grit to compost
temp	Grow in warm greenhouse conditions, with a minimum temperature of 13°C (55°F)
water & humidity	Keep fairly dry after planting and water well once in growth. Reduce until dry by late autumn
general care	Tubers should be removed from compost once dormant and stored in a dry place until spring planting time
pests & diseases	Aphids can be a problem. Over watering at the wrong time of year can cause rots. but few other problems

Guzmania

Guzmania is one of the bromeliads that is grown both for its brightly coloured, showy flowerheads and for its architectural foliage. As with all the bromeliads, it is easy to care for, but it does require more warmth and a higher humidity than most of the others.

The plant consists of a rosette of thick, glossy, dark green leaves which look good year round. In late spring and summer, a flower spike is produced. However, it is the colourful bracts that surround the true flowers that are the most spectacular part. In the case of *Guzmania lingulata*, which is the easiest to look after and the most attractive of the guzmanias, these can be in any shade of red, pink or orange. The true flowers are white and are produced in the centre of a rosette of colourful bracts. They quickly fade but the bracts provide an impressive, long-lasting display. *Guzmania musaica* bears a red flower, but it is the large, variegated, banded foliage that the plant is grown for.

To keep guzmanias healthy, the most important factor is to ensure is that they have a constantly high humidity. Misting the plant every day will help, as will grouping it with other humidity lovers and regularly damping down the greenhouse or conservatory. The plant should be watered via the central vase formed by the rosette of leaves. From spring to autumn this should always be kept full, and in winter it should be kept half full. This should ensure that the compost is always slightly moist.

After flowering, the main plant will die. If you want to continue growing it you will need to propagate soon after flowering. Small offsets will be produced at the side of the main plant. When these are large enough and have formed root systems of their own they can be prised from the plant and potted up in fresh compost. The new plant will eventually flower if kept in the correct conditions.

Guzmania lingulata

soil	Requires an open but peaty compost of equal parts peat, leaf mould and grit
temp	Grow in a hot greenhouse or conservatory. Minimum temperature of 16°C (61°F)
water & humidity	High humidity so mist daily. Water well in summer by filling the plant's central vase; reduce in winter
general care	The main plant will die after flowering, so it is essential to propagate from offshoots after each flowering
pests & diseases	Scale insect and mealy bug. Brown tips to leaves can indicate that humidity is too low or watering insufficient

Guzmania lingulata

	SPRING	SUMMER	AUTUMN	WINTER	height (cm)	spread (cm)	flower colour	
Guzmania lingulata					30	45		Flowers of this plant have variable colouring
G. musaica					50	70		Attractively variegated leaves

- flowering

Hatiora
Easter cactus

Hatiora rosea is the plant commonly known as the Easter cactus, due to its flowering time. In early and mid-spring it is covered in beautifully bold pink flowers. Its relative, H. gaertneri, produces bright red flowers at about the same time.

The stems of the plants are fairly attractive in their own right. They are formed from a number of joined, flattened segments. They are mid-green and can turn slightly reddish in colour in high light levels. This suggests that they are receiving too much direct sunlight. They do need bright light, but it should be filtered if possible and they should be shaded from the heat of the midday summer sun. This is indicative of the fact that these are not like most cacti, which originate in desert-like environments. Hatiora is among a group of plants known as forest cacti. In the wild they are often epiphytic, meaning that they will grow in cracks on branches. They will also grow on the forest floor. Because of this they like an open, freely draining soil containing leaf mould and some shade to recreate their natural conditions.

soil	Suitable compost is made of a mixture of leaf mould and a good multi-purpose compost
temp	Warm greenhouse or conservatory, minimum temperature of 10°C (50°F)
water & humidity	Water well from mid-winter until autumn and keep almost dry in winter. High humidity so mist daily
general care	Plants need complete rest in winter. From winter until early spring artificial light at night can prevent flowering
pests & diseases	Mealy bug can be a problem. Brown spots indicate too low temperatures, and red stems that light levels are too high

Hatioras like a fair amount of moisture during the growing season and will enjoy high humidity, particularly in summer. They should be watered well and fed from the time they begin flowering until after flowering is over. They will respond well to being placed outside during summer as long as they are in a fairly shady spot. Make sure that you continue to water them during dry spells. However, it is essential to allow them to dry out in winter if you want to get them to flower again. Start this process in autumn by gradually reducing the amount of water you give them until they are almost completely dry. Keep them this way until mid-winter, when you can begin careful watering again. During their resting time, keep them in a spot that is not lit at night, as this can disturb their flowering pattern and lead to them not flowering in spring.

Hatiora 'City of Aberdeen'

	SPRING	SUMMER	AUTUMN	WINTER	height (cm)	spread (cm)	flower colour
Hatiora 'City of Aberdeen'	● ● ●				15	25	Slender, tube-shaped light pink flowers
H. gaertneri	● ● ●				15	25	Red flowers on mid-green stems
H. rosea	● ●				15	15	The Easter cactus with bright pink flowers

● *flowering*

Hedera
Ivy

The ivies are attractive foliage plants that can be grown as climbers or trailers. There are a huge variety of leaf shapes, sizes and colours available that make them useful in many different situations.

Hedera helix 'Goldchild'

In their natural habitat, ivies are climbers. They use strong aerial roots to grip onto surfaces and pull themselves up. They will need supports to climb up and can be trained around interesting shapes such as spirals or circles. The lax stems should be loosely tied in to the chosen support in order to encourage them to grip on properly. Trellis, wire frames, canes and moss poles can all be used as effective supports.

Because of the lax habit of their stems they also make great trailing plants. Grow them in a hanging basket or in a pot on a shelf to show off the stems. Plants that are particularly suitable to grow as trailers include the more compact cultivars such as *Hedera helix* 'Ivalace' and *H. helix* 'Little Diamond'.

Ivies are hardy, and many that are commonly grown as conservatory and greenhouse plants are just as happy when grown outside. This helps to indicate the kind of conditions that they will need. Grow in cool temperatures, as they tend to suffer if kept too warm, particularly over winter. It is important that the variegated types have good light, as the leaves will begin to revert to green and to lose their variegation in low light. Mist regularly, particularly in warm conditions in summer, and ventilate well. You can also try placing plants in a shady spot outside for a while during summer months, making sure the plant is well watered at all times.

When buying, look for plants with several stems. Encourage a multi-branching

Hedera canariensis 'Gloire de Marengo'

habit by occasionally cutting back old stems and pruning tips of the younger stems. As stems get older they will lose leaves at the base. If your plant has plenty of young stems, remove the older ones when this starts to happen.

soil	Will perform best if planted into a good, multi-purpose compost
temp	Grow in cool greenhouse conditions, with a minimum temperature of 2°C (36°F)
water & humidity	Water normally in summer, less in winter. High summer humidity, normal humidity the rest of the year
general care	If growing as a climber, provide a support and tie shoots in to it regularly. Prune if growing too large
pests & diseases	Aphids, red spider mite, scale insects. Brown leaf tips or edges occur with warm temperatures or low humidity

	SPRING	SUMMER	AUTUMN	WINTER	height (cm)	spread (cm)	flower colour	
Hedera canariensis 'Gloire de Marengo'			● ● ● / ● ● ●		200	80		Large variegated climber
H. helix			● ● ● / ● ● ●		150	45		Vigorous climber
H. helix 'Fluffy Ruffles'			● ● ● / ● ● ●		80	25		Attractive frilled edges to the leaves
H. helix 'Goldchild'			● ● ● / ● ● ●		80	35		Bold yellow variegation
H. helix 'Ivalace'			● ● ● / ● ● ●		80	35		Curled edges to leaves
H. helix 'Little Diamond'			● ● ● / ● ● ●		30	15		Extremely compact variegated plant

● *flowering*

H

Conservatory & Greenhouse Plants

Hedychium
Ginger lily

Hedychiums are related to the culinary ginger, Zingiber. They have particularly exotic looking leaves and flowers. The leaves are large and tropical looking, and appear from chunky rhizomes planted in the ground

Hedychium 'Assam Orange'

From the centre of these clumps of leaves arise tall spikes of flowers. The flower spikes are made up of many small, almost orchid-like flowers, which are arranged cylindrically around the spike. These flowers are most often found in shades of cream through to light orange, but occasionally have some red or dark orange parts.

Many hedychiums are almost hardy, and can be grown out of doors in areas that receive only light frosts. However, to be sure that they will survive and grow well in any temperate climate, it is a good idea to grow them with a little protection, at least in winter. A cold house will most probably offer adequate protection from the harshest winter frosts, but they will really thrive in a cool house that is kept at a temperature just above freezing all winter.

Grow them in normal multi-purpose compost and keep them in a spot that receives good filtered light, and where they will be shaded from the heat of any direct

soil	Will perform best if planted into a good, multi-purpose compost
temp	Grow all of these hedychiums in cold or cool greenhouse conditions
water & humidity	Water well in summer, keep almost dry in winter. Needs high humidity, particularly in warm weather in summer
general care	Hedychium plants can appreciate being planted out of doors for a spell during the summer
pests & diseases	Aphids and red spider mite can both cause problems on Hedychium plants, particularly in low humidity

Hedychium gardnerianum

Hedychium coccineum 'Tara'

midday sun. They require good ventilation in summer, particularly on warm summer days and should receive high levels of humidity over this time. A good alternative is to move them outdoors over summer and place them in light dappled shade, ensuring they are well watered, particularly during dry spells. There they will put on good growth and can even be left to flower there. Alternatively, bring them into the greenhouse or conservatory to enjoy the flowers. Move them indoors before any frost is forecast.

	SPRING	SUMMER	AUTUMN	WINTER	height (cm)	spread (cm)	flower colour	
Hedychium coccineum 'Tara'		●	●		300	100		Striking colouring to exotic flowers
H. coronarium		● ●			300	100		Scented pale flowers
H. densiflorum 'Assam Orange'		●	●		500	200		Closely packed spikes of dark orange flowers
H. gardnerianum		●	●		200	100		Bold yellow variegation

● *flowering*

Hibiscus

The large flowers of Hibiscus have a striking shape and are available in almost every colour and shade. They make great looking plants that are fairly easy to look after, and are extremely free flowering.

It is the cultivars of a particular species, *Hibiscus rosa-sinensis*, which are most commonly grown. This species has the common name rose of China after its country of origin. It has dark, glossy leaves and large, bright red flowers and makes a fantastic plant for a conservatory or warm greenhouse. The cultivars all have the same glossy leaves, and have a wide variation in flower colour and type. The best colours

Hibiscus rosa-sinensis 'Rose'

tend to be the dark reds and oranges. *H. rosa-sinensis* 'Cairo' has flowers in shades of orange, pink and apricot that are shown off by dark glossy foliage. *H. rosa-sinensis* 'Rose' has pink flowers and bright green foliage.

Hibiscus is usually thought of as a conservatory plant, because it likes lots of light and a fair bit of direct sunlight, as well as quite a high temperature. However, even hibiscus will not tolerate the heat of the

midday sun in summer, so be sure to provide some shade. They need plenty of water in summer and will benefit from regular misting to maintain moderate humidity. They could also be grouped with other humidity loving plants and should be in a greenhouse or conservatory that is regularly damped down in warm weather.

Plants can grow quite large, so it is important to train them regularly to keep them at a manageable size. In late winter, cut the stems back by up to half. Flowers will be formed on the fresh growth that is produced in spring.

A particular problem hibiscus plants can suffer from is flower-bud drop. This tends to happen if plants have been allowed to dry out and have had low humidity, or if they have been moved or had a sudden change in temperature.

soil	Will perform best if planted into a good, multi-purpose compost
temp	Grow in warm greenhouse conditions with minimum temperature of 10°C (50°F)
water & humidity	Water well in summer and reduce watering in winter. Moderate humidity. Mist when temperatures are high
general care	Ensure good ventilation in summer. Prune in late winter to keep the plant small and bushy
pests & diseases	Aphids, red spider mite, whitefly, powdery mildew, scale insects. Temperature drop causes flower-bud drop

	SPRING	SUMMER	AUTUMN	WINTER	height (cm)	spread (cm)	flower colour	
Hibiscus rosa-sinensis		● ● ●	● ● ●		250	150		Easy to grow plant
H. rosa-sinensis 'Cairo'		● ● ●	● ● ●		250	150		Dark glossy foliage shows off flowers
H. rosa-sinensis 'Rose'		● ● ●	● ● ●		250	150		Bright-green, glossy leaves

● *flowering*

Hippeastrum

Amaryllis

The flowers of Hippeastrum are a mid-winter treat. Borne at the tops of erect flower stems, they can be anything up to 15cm (6in) across and are available in a wide range of colours.

Three outer petals contain three slightly smaller inner petals, giving the flower an almost triangular shape when viewed from the front, and a trumpet shape when viewed from the side. Each flower spike can carry three of these impressive blooms.

Hippeastrum, which is often more commonly known as amaryllis, is usually bought as a bulb in autumn or winter and potted up. Plants that are in flower or are about to flower can also be bought, but these will be more expensive. Bulbs that have been treated for early flowering are bought in autumn and flower in winter. They will often flower in mid-winter. Untreated bulbs are usually planted in winter for early spring flowering.

Buy a pot that the bulb fits into with just an inch or two of space on either side and pot it up so that half of the bulb is above the surface of the compost. Place in a warm spot and keep almost dry until growth appears. You should then increase watering. The flower spike of prepared bulbs will appear after a few weeks, while unprepared bulbs may take up to eight weeks to flower.

After flowering the flower spike will gradually die off and should then be removed. Keep feeding and watering until the leaves start to die down. Then gradually give the bulb less water and food until it has completely died down. If the leaves do not die down of their own accord, cutting back on food and water encourages dormancy.

Only pot bulbs on after several years, as they resent disturbance. Offsets will eventually be formed, and these can be grown on to flowering size, although this can take several years.

soil	Will perform best if planted into a good, multi-purpose compost
temp	Grow hippeastrum in warm greenhouse. Minimum temperature 13°C (55°F)
water & humidity	Water carefully as growth starts and well when flowering. Keep dry in winter. Moderate humidity
general care	Bulbs should be potted up with about half the bulb above the compost. Only re-pot after 3–5 years
pests & diseases	Red spider mite, thrips, mealy bug and some fungal diseases. Non-flowering can be caused by lack of feeding

Hippeastrum hybrida

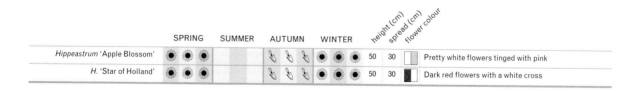

	SPRING	SUMMER	AUTUMN	WINTER	height (cm)	spread (cm)	flower colour	
Hippeastrum 'Apple Blossom'	●●●			●●●	50	30		Pretty white flowers tinged with pink
H. 'Star of Holland'	●●●			●●●	50	30		Dark red flowers with a white cross

planting ● flowering

Howea forsteriana

Kentia palm

Howea makes a great impact as a tall, graceful specimen. Over several years it matures into a big and beautiful plant that will command attention in any greenhouse or conservatory.

Howea forsteriana is commonly known as the Kentia palm. Kentia is the capital of Lord Howe Island off the coast of Australia, the only place these palms are found in the wild. When grown as a conservatory plant it reaches up to 3m (10ft) in height with large, arching fronds.

Howea has some fairly exacting requirements, but once these are fulfilled it is pretty straightforward to care for. It needs a deep root run, so make sure you give it a good, deep pot. It also must be planted into an acidic compost – any labelled as ericaceous or lime free should be suitable. Take care to always water with soft water. If you live in a hard water area, collect fresh rainwater and use this to irrigate Howea plants. Take care not to over water all year round, and especially in winter, but do keep the compost slightly moist at all times. Alkaline soil, hard water and poor drainage will all lead to brown tips developing on the plants. Put a layer of crocks or other drainage in the bottom of the pot to prevent the drainage holes from clogging up with compost.

They also have a need for fairly high temperatures, making them more suitable as a conservatory plant, unless you are able to sustain warm greenhouse temperatures. In winter, however, it is important to keep their night temperature below 14°C (57°F). Howea plants require average to high humidity levels depending on the temperature, so take care to mist them or regularly damp down nearby in warm summer weather.

When plants are small they can be kept in quite shady spots, underneath other plants or towards the back of conservatories, mirroring the conditions young seedlings grow under at the bottom of the canopy in the wild. As plants grow larger they will need higher levels of light, but it should always be filtered and they should not be left in direct sunlight as it would scorch the leaves.

As plants age, the larger, lower fronds will turn brown and die back. This is part of the plant's natural growth process and is nothing to be alarmed at. They should be cut away close to the base of the plant.

Propagation is difficult as seed will only germinate at high temperatures.

soil	Will grow best in a deep pot filled with well-drained ericaceous compost
temp	Grow in warm greenhouse conditions with a minimum temperature of 10°C (50°F)
water & humidity	Water normally in summer and sparingly in winter using soft water. Average humidity. Sponge leaves occasionally
general care	Grow in bright filtered light or light shade. Do not use leaf shine products as they will harm the leaves
pests & diseases	Red spider mites, scale insects, mealy bugs. Brown tips or edges caused by hard water or alkaline compost

Howea forsteriana

Hoya

Hoyas are shrubby specimens that are popular as greenhouse and conservatory plants for their heads of thick, waxy flowers, some of which produce a beautiful scent in the evening and during the night.

There are two hoyas that are commonly grown. *Hoya carnosa* is the most popular. It grows rather large, reaching around 3m (10ft) in height very quickly. Its long, lax stems will need to be supported by training them to a support. A trellis is suitable, but it does climb by means of aerial roots and so can be easily grown up a moss pole. It produces round heads of small, solid flowers that are pink in colour with a red centre. These are strongly night scented.

Hoya carnosa

The other Hoya commonly grown as a conservatory or greenhouse plant is *H. lanceolata* subsp. *bella*. This is a smaller plant, reaching just 45cm (18in) in height and spread, and so is far more suitable for the space most people have available. However, it is not so popular as *H. carnosa*, partly because it is not so floriferous. It has round heads of small, white waxy flowers.

It is important that hoyas are grown in a well-drained ericaceous compost and that they are watered with soft water to prevent the compost from turning alkaline. Use tap water if you live in a soft water area, but use freshly collected rainwater if you live in a hard water area. Make sure you use ericaceous compost whenever you pot the plants on, which should be every three years or so, and when you top dress the plant every spring.

Plants should be watered well all summer and watering should continue in winter, but at a much lower rate. Make sure the compost is kept just moist in winter. Provide high humidity in summer by damping down and misting regularly, particularly in hot weather.

soil	Best in a well-drained mixture of ericaceous compost, bark and charcoal
temp	Grow Hoya in cool greenhouse conditions, 7°C (45°F) minimum temperature
water & humidity	Water well in summer and keep soil moist in winter. High humidity so mist and damp down regularly
general care	*Hoya carnosa* grows large and should be tied into a support such as a trellis or moss pole
pests & diseases	Scale insects, mealy bugs and aphids all attack Hoya plants. Leaves turn yellow in lime-containing compost

	SPRING	SUMMER	AUTUMN	WINTER	height (cm)	spread (cm)	flower colour	
Hoya carnosa		● ● ●			300	200	▨	Solid waxy flowers are scented at night
H. lanceolata subsp. *bella*	●	● ● ●			45	45	☐	Compact plant with white flowers

● *flowering*

Impatiens
Busy lizzie

Impatiens are easy and rewarding plants to grow for use in greenhouses or conservatories. Many will provide a great display of brightly coloured flowers through summer, and will then flower intermittently through the rest of the year.

Some impatiens also have attractively variegated and coloured leaves that complement the flower colour.

They are short-lived plants, and many are best treated as annuals and replaced after a year. This is not really much of a hardship, as tip cuttings take extremely easily and quickly grow into plants of flowering size. If you are keeping old plants, cut them back fairly hard each spring to produce a flush of new growth. Pinch the tips out regularly to keep the plant compact and bushy.

Care is straightforward. Give plenty of light and water in summer and mist the leaves occasionally. One of the few problems to beset impatiens is flower bud drop. This can occur if the compost is allowed to dry or the humidity around the plant is too low. In winter, continue watering moderately.

The classic busy lizzies are the cultivars of *Impatiens walleriana*. Modern breeding has led to the development of compact plants. These mounds of foliage can be covered in large flowers in a wide range of colours including pink, red, orange, purple and white.

soil	Will perform best if planted into a good, multi-purpose compost
temp	Grow in warm greenhouse conditions. Minimum temperature 10°C (50°F)
water & humidity	Water freely in active growth, and sparingly in winter. Requires normal winter humidity
general care	Regularly pinch out the tips of growing stems to prevent leggy bare stems developing and to keep the plant bushy
pests & diseases	Red spider mite is a problem in low humidity; botrytis in damp conditions. Vine weevil and aphids

The New Guinea hybrids are a relatively recent development. They form larger, more robust plants than the busy lizzies and many have attractive, coloured foliage. Their flowers are larger than those of *I. walleriana*. Both *I. walleriana* hybrids and New Guinea hybrids can either be grown in a greenhouse or conservatory, or can be started off in a greenhouse and planted out as bedding as soon as all danger of frost has passed.

I. niamniamensis 'Congo Cockatoo' is a bit of a curiosity. It forms groups of brightly coloured, pouch-shaped flowers that hang beneath the leaf joints. The name comes from the strange shape and red and yellow colouring of the flowers. When clustered under the leaves they are reminiscent of brightly coloured tropical birds. It makes an attractive and unusual indoor plant.

Impatiens New Guinea hybrids

Impatiens niamniamensis 'Congo Cockatoo'

	SPRING	SUMMER	AUTUMN	WINTER	height (cm)	spread (cm)	flower colour	
Impatiens New Guinea hybrids		● ● ●	● ● ●		60	60	▌▌▌	Good foliage and flowers in a wide range of colours
I. niamniamensis 'Congo Cockatoo'	● ● ●	● ● ●	● ● ●	● ● ●	90	35	▌	Quirky flowers produced all year
I. walleriana cultivars	● ● ●	● ● ●	● ● ●	● ● ●	30	30	▌▌▌	The classic busy lizzie

● *flowering*

Iris

Irises are widely known as good garden plants. However, there are some species that are not suitable for growing out of doors in most temperate climates, and these can be grown in an alpine house or in a cool greenhouse.

These are not plants that need the extra heat provided by being grown under glass in order to grow well. In fact they will take extremely low temperatures. They do have a problem with the amount of rainfall they would receive over an average winter, and growing them in a greenhouse provides the protection they need from winter wet, preventing their roots and stems from rotting away. They will appreciate being grown in an extremely well drained compost, so mix one part horticultural grit with one part multi-purpose compost.

As you might expect, therefore, they do not require any artificial heat. They should be grown in a cold house that receives no heating at all, even over winter. In fact, they will suffer if the temperature gets too high. Make sure the house they are grown in is extremely well ventilated and that vents and windows are all opened as soon as the temperature starts to rise in spring. They may even need to be opened on warm winter days. If growing alpines it may be a good idea to invest in a fan that will move cold air around throughout the year and keep the plants well ventilated, preventing too much moisture from gathering in the house.

If you provide these conditions, it will make it hard to grow any plants that require warmth or shelter from frost in your greenhouse. If you want to grow these plants you will have to decide to set your greenhouse up as a dedicated alpine house. Other plants, such as bulbs, can be grown in these conditions, but they will primarily suit alpines.

Iris reticulata cultivar

Iris reticulata cultivar

soil		Will grow best if planted into a multi-purpose compost with added grit
temp		Grow irises in cold greenhouse conditions or in an alpine house
water & humidity		Water normally while in active growth, and sparingly in winter, keeping soil just moist. Low humidity
general care		Ventilation is critical to their health and they may need moving outdoors during summer
pests & diseases		These irises are fairly trouble free and do not suffer from any particular problems with pests and diseases

	SPRING	SUMMER	AUTUMN	WINTER	height (cm)	spread (cm)	flower colour	
Iris magnifica	● ●				40	30	▮▮▮	Iris in pale pastel colours
I. reticulata	●			●	15	10	▮▮▮	Small, fragrant flowers with striking colouring
I. 'White Wedgwood'	● ● ●	● ●			65	40	▮▮▮	Iris with pale colouring

● *flowering*

Jasminum polyanthum

Jasmine

The delicate, twining stems of *Jasminum polyanthum* produce masses of tiny, star-shaped, white flowers throughout winter and spring. The plant is widely grown for the scent of the flowers, which is at its strongest in the evening.

Jasmine is a climbing plant, and left unsupported the weak stems would not make for an attractive plant. However, it is easy to train into any shape. The most common way is to train it over a hoop of wire, but it is a vigorous plant and will take on pretty much any form you care to train it into. Once you have chosen a support, carefully tie the stems into it using soft garden twine. As the stems grow, they will need regular tying in. Jasmine can grow quite large, up to around 3m (10ft) in height. It can make an impressive plant when grown to this size in a greenhouse or cool conservatory, and would look good trained up a pillar, across a wall or along the ridge of a greenhouse roof.

The flowers are produced from late autumn into spring. While many welcome the scent of jasmine flowers, be warned that some find it a little overpowering when the plant is grown in a confined space. The scent is particularly strong in the evening and at night.

Old stems will eventually stop producing flowers, so it is important to prune out old growth occasionally. Do this soon after flowering has finished in early spring. New flowers are always formed on the previous year's growth, so be sure to leave plenty of this growth on the plant when you prune or you will have to wait a whole year for your next batch of flowers.

soil	This plant will grow well if planted into a multi-purpose compost
temp	Grow in warm greenhouse conditions with a minimum temperature of 13°C (55°F)
water & humidity	Water well in active growth, keeping compost moist, sparingly in winter. Mist leaves in summer
general care	Regular tying in of stems is necessary. Prune out old growth, one-year-old growth is most floriferous.
pests & diseases	Aphids, mealy bugs, red spider mite and scale insects. Lack of nutrients cause leaves to drop

Feeding in summer should be with a low-nitrogen fertilizer. This is to prevent the plant from putting too much energy into non-flowering, green shoots, and to encourage it to put its energy into flower production. During summer it can also be placed out of doors for a spell if the weather is warm. Find a lightly shaded spot and keep the plant well watered.

Suckers will often arise from near the base of the plant, and these make propagation simple. They should be removed, preferably in spring when re-potting the plant, and potted up in fresh compost.

It is also easy to propagate the plant from layering. Take a young stem of the plant and pin it down into a pot of compost, covering it with more compost. This shoot will soon take root and it can then be cut from the parent plant.

Jasminum polyanthum

Justicia

Justicia is commonly grown as a houseplant, but it is far happier and much more impressive grown in the heat, light and space offered by a conservatory or greenhouse. They can make impressive shrub-like plants that will flower almost all year round if allowed to.

Justicia carnea

The most popular variety is possibly the most impressive. *Justicia brandegeeana* is commonly known as the shrimp plant, because of the shape and colour of its flowers. they are made up of a series of pink bracts that overlap and form the shape of a shrimp. The shade changes slightly from the base of the flower to the tip to give a lovely graduation of colour from pink through to pale yellow. The true flowers are white and poke out from the ends of the tubes of bracts. If planted out into a conservatory or greenhouse border, or into a large pot, this plant can reach up to 1m (3ft) in height. If the tips are pinched out regularly it will form a good rounded shape. Although it will flower all year round, it is a good idea to force it into a period of rest over winter by cutting back on watering. If allowed to flower all year round, it may burn itself out.

J. rizzinii is not too different in habit and requirements. It stays smaller in height and spread, and produces small, tubular flowers in bright red and yellow.

J. carnea is slightly different. It produces large heads of bright pink flowers on the ends of its stems and grows fairly large. It is also more fussy than the other two plants, really preferring slightly warmer temperatures and higher humidity. Its compost should never

soil	This plant will grow well if planted into a multi-purpose compost
temp	Grow in cool greenhouse conditions with a minimum temperature of 7°C (45°F)
water & humidity	Water well in summer, less in winter. Low humidity for *J. brandegeeana* and *J. rizzinii*, high for *J. carnea*
general care	Nip out the tips of the stems of all these plants as they are growing to encourage bushy and compact growth
pests & diseases	Red spider mite, aphids and whitefly can all attack and cause problems for plants of Justicia

be left to dry out during summer but should be kept constantly moist.

All justicias appreciate fairly high light levels, but they should have some shade from direct midday sun, apart from in the winter.

Justicia rizzinii

	SPRING	SUMMER	AUTUMN	WINTER	height (cm)	spread (cm)	flower colour	
Justicia brandegeeana	● ● ●	● ● ●	● ● ●	● ● ●	100	80		Grows into a floriferous shrubby plant
J. carnea		● ● ●	● ● ●		200	100		Clusters of pink flowers on the ends of shoots
J. rizzinii	● ● ●		● ● ●	● ● ●	50	50		Freely produced red and yellow tube shaped flowers

● *flowering*

Kalanchoe

There are a number of different Kalanchoe species that can be grown in a greenhouse or conservatory. All have succulent stems and leaves and some have colourful flowers. The most popular is *Kalanchoe blossfeldiana* and its cultivars.

The species produces bright red flowers that last for several weeks on top of mid-green succulent leaves. The cultivars are available in a number of flower colours, including purple and yellow. It is popular as a Christmas flowering plant. After flowering, many people simply throw them away and buy new plants the following year. If you want to keep your plant it should be given a period of rest for around six weeks. *Kalanchoe manginii* also produces red flowers on trailing, succulent stems. It can be grown in a hanging basket or on the edge of a shelf where its stems can hang freely. Although the other kalanchoes produce flowers, most are grown for their foliage.

As succulents, these plants require low humidity and fairly low levels of water. They need good light and even some direct summer sun – as much direct light as possible during winter. Grow them in cacti and succulent compost, which contains large amounts of grit. This enables water to drain through the compost faster, and prevents it from sitting near the roots and making them rot. Create

Kalanchoe blossfeldiana

your own cacti and succulent compost by mixing a large amount of grit into some multi-purpose compost.

Feed plants once a month during summer, using a liquid feed. Reduce feeding towards autumn. Kalanchoes sometimes produce offsets. These can be carefully teased away from the main plant and potted up. Propagate also from seed in a heated propagator in spring.

soil	Well-drained cacti compost or a multi-purpose compost with added grit
temp	Warm greenhouse conditions. Minimum temperature 12°C (54°F)
water & humidity	Water fairly well but carefully in summer and keep just moist in winter. Require low humidity
general care	Reduce watering to almost nothing and allow these plants to rest for about one month after flowering
pests & diseases	Aphids, mealy bugs and mildew can all attack and cause problems on Kalanchoe plants

Kalanchoe manginii

	SPRING	SUMMER	AUTUMN	WINTER	height (cm)	spread (cm)	flower colour	
Kalanchoe blossfeldiana	●			●	60	30	■	Grown for its showy flowers
K. manginii	● ● ●				30	30	■	Plant has a trailing habit

● *flowering*

Conservatory & Greenhouse Plants

Lachenalia

Bulbs such as Lachenalia rate pretty highly among the delights available to the greenhouse and conservatory owner. They produce exquisitely coloured flowers on attractively mottled stems at an often dull time of year. Some are even scented.

Lachenalias do not require high levels of heat. However, it is most probably a good idea to keep them in a cool greenhouse where the temperature is kept above freezing, rather than in a cold greenhouse. They can be bought as bulbs in summer and should be planted out into a multi-purpose compost with a little incorporated peat in late summer. Plant them with the tips just below the surface of the compost. Growth will gradually start to show and they should be watered carefully at first. As more growth appears, watering can be increased and occasional feeding should start.

The green leaves, mottled with brown and purple marks will appear first and from them will arise the flower stems, similarly

soil	Plant into multi-purpose compost with a little peat incorporated into it
temp	Grow in cool greenhouse conditions with a minimum temperature of 7°C (45°F)
water & humidity	Increase watering gradually as bulbs start to grow. Cut back as bulb dies down. Average humidity
general care	Once foliage has died down keep bulbs completely dry until it is time to re-plant in late summer
pests & diseases	Lachenalia plants are fairly free of major problems with any particular pests or diseases

Lachenalia aloides var. quadricolor

attractively patterned. Over this time it is essential that they receive high levels of light, but they should not be allowed to get too warm. Ventilate the area well in warm weather.

After flowering, you will need to gradually reduce the amount of water and feed you are giving the plants to help encourage them to die down. The leaves will gradually die back. Once they have done so, the bulbs can be lifted and stored. Propagate at this time from any small bulbils that have formed. Re-plant bulbs and new bulbils in late summer and begin the process again.

Lachenalia bulbs can be tricky to track down as they are not widely grown. Try contacting a specialist bulb grower or supplier if you are unable to find any in a garden centre.

	SPRING	SUMMER	AUTUMN	WINTER	height (cm)	spread (cm)	flower colour	
Lachenalia aloides var. *aurea*	●	✎		● ● ●	20	5		Blotched stems and yellow-orange flowers
L. aloides var. *quadricolor*	●	✎		● ● ●	20	5		Flowers open red and age to yellow
L. orchioides var. *glaucina*	● ●	✎		●	15	5		Blue and purple shades to flowers

✎ planting   ● flowering

Lapageria
Chilean bellflower

Among the many beautiful climbers that can be grown in conservatories and greenhouses, Lapageria can hold its own. It produces bold, waxy, soft red flowers that hang down from among its glossy, dark green evergreen leaves.

Lapageria rosea cultivar

Lapageria is almost hardy, but performs best in the shelter afforded by growing under glass. It does not need high temperatures and should ideally be grown in cool house temperatures – a greenhouse or conservatory that is kept just frost free is perfect. Ventilation is important, particularly during warm weather. High humidity is required in the run up to flowering, so damp down the floor and benches near to the plant regularly from late spring onwards.

The stems climb by twining around supports. It is a large plant, and so it is important to provide a sturdy support for it to grow up. Attach horizontal wires to a wall or erect a solid trellis. If possible, try to train the plant so that it grows overhead, perhaps by growing it along the ridge of a greenhouse or conservatory. This allows the flowers to hang down below the foliage and means that they are shown off to their best.

As these plants can grow so large, you may need to prune them occasionally to keep them down to size. Do this in early spring, when new growth is just starting. Take out any thin spindly stems and any damaged ones first and then cut the rest back to fit the space you have available.

Lapageria plants are lime-haters and so they must be grown in ericaceous compost. Make sure you continue to use ericaceous compost when potting on and top dressing. Using soft water when watering will help prevent the compost from turning alkaline. If you live in a hard water area, collect fresh rainwater and use that.

Lapageria rosea cultivar

soil	Any well-drained compost or in a greenhouse or conservatory border
temp	Cool house conditions are suitable if a minimum 7°C (45°F) is maintained
water & humidity	Average watering and humidity required. Water well during summer and carefully during winter
general care	In spring, prune the previous year's growth back by roughly half to encourage bushy growth in summer
pests & diseases	Can suffer from pests such as whitefly, greenfly, scale insects, mealy bugs and red spider mite

	SPRING	SUMMER	AUTUMN	WINTER	height (cm)	spread (cm)	flower colour	
Lapageria rosea		● ● ●	● ● ●		500	250	■	Waxy red flowers hang down from stem
L. rosea var. albiflora		● ● ●	● ● ●		500	250	□	White flowered plant

● *flowering*

Lewisia

Lewisia is an alpine plant that produces large heads of colourful flowers, originating mainly from the western North American region. It forms a rosette of evergreen leaves, which looks good even before it flowers.

Among alpine plants, Lewisia is surprisingly colourful. Alpines usually have tiny, delicately coloured flowers, and many alpine growers prefer these shrinking violets to the more obvious charms of other plants.

The hybrids of *Lewisia cotyledon* can therefore look a little brash when compared to other alpines, but many people love the splash of colour they bring to an alpine house. Flower spikes appear from the centre of a rosette of leaves. At the tops of these stems appears a group of many large flowers in shades of pink, orange and yellow. If you want to grow Lewisia but find these hybrids too bold, try growing *L. tweedyi*. This Lewisia is also evergreen and forms a rosette of leaves, but the flowers it produces are in a beautifully clear pale pink. They also have a simpler shape than the hybrid. They are still showy among alpine plants, but have far more of the understated beauty that is normally associated with the group.

Lewisia cotyledon

Alpines are grown in a greenhouse not because they require extra heat, but because they need shelter from moisture. In an average temperate winter the roots of most alpines would simply rot away. If they are kept out of the rain and damp they can take extremely low temperatures. Therefore it is essential that you have an unheated greenhouse if you are going to grow these plants. It should also be well ventilated, and may even contain a fan to move cool air around.

To encourage water to drain away from the roots, it is a good idea to incorporate some grit into the compost. However, these plants will also appreciate having a little leaf mould added to the compost mix.

soil	Grow in a compost with leaf-mould and grit incorporated into it
temp	Grow in an alpine house or in cold greenhouse conditions
water & humidity	Water this plant fairly well in summer and keep it almost dry in winter. Requires a low humidity
general care	To propagate sow seed in autumn. Propagate hybrids of Lewisia cotyledon by removing small offsets
pests & diseases	Aphids can attack and cause problems for Lewisia plants. Over watering can lead to rotting of stems

Lewisia cotyledon

	SPRING	SUMMER	AUTUMN	WINTER	height (cm)	spread (cm)	flower colour	
Lewisia cotyledon hybrids	●	● ● ●			20	30	▊	Heads of many boldly coloured flowers
L. tweedyi	● ●	●			20	30	▊	Delicately coloured open flowers

● *flowering*

Mammillaria

Mammillaria species are among the most popular and widely grown of all cacti. This is mainly because they are fairly easy to grow well and to encourage to flower. Unlike some cacti, many Mammillaria species will flower while they are young.

Mammillaria baumii

Mammillaria bocosana

Mammillaria bombycina

Mammillarias gradually clump up and will fill a pot over several years. The flowers are usually borne in a ring around the top of the plant. They are produced in a range of colours including bright pink, yellow and white. After the flowers have faded they are sometimes followed by small pointed berries, which are almost as ornamental.

There are a number of different shapes and forms, as well as differences in the arrangement of the spines. Some of the most interesting are those covered with a layer of fine, white spines, giving the impression of a layer of fluff covering the whole plant. One of the best examples of this is *Mammillaria bocosana*, which is commonly known as the snowball cactus because of its round habit and fluff of spines. *M. bombycina* is even more thickly covered in fine white spines. Larger, brown, hooked spines poke out from the fine covering.

Many people are surprised at the amount of water cacti require to grow well. It is true that they will survive on dribbles of water, often for many years, but for them to grow and flower at their best you will need to water and feed them regularly throughout summer. They should, however, be left almost completely dry over winter. Give them a small amount of water occasionally, or if you notice any shrivelling of the plant.

It is important to grow cacti in high light levels. They will not thrive and will almost certainly fail to flower if they are kept in shade. It is also important to clean them regularly with a soft brush. Dust can gather on the surface of the plant and cut down on the amount of light they receive. Use a soft brush to carefully remove any dust.

soil	Will grow best if planted into a gritty, well-drained, cacti and succulent compost
temp	Grow in cool greenhouse conditions with a minimum temperature of 7°C (45°F)
water & humidity	Water these plants well in summer and keep almost dry in winter. Require a low humidity
general care	Take care when re-potting as spines can be painful. Wear gloves and wrap the stem in a piece of newspaper
pests & diseases	Mealy bugs can attack and cause problems for Mammillaria plants. Flowers may not form in low light

	SPRING	SUMMER	AUTUMN	WINTER	height (cm)	spread (cm)	flower colour	
Mammillaria baumii		● ●			8	12		Fine white spines over plant
M. bocosana	● ●	● ●			5	30		Whole plant has a hairy texture
M. bombycina		● ●			20	30		Has dramatically hooked spines
M. hahniana		● ●			15	30		Dense bristles cover the plants

● *flowering*

Maranta

Marantas have broad, oval leaves that are often velvety in texture. They are boldly patterned with stripes and blotches in colours including brown, pale yellowy-green, bright red and a green so dark it could easily pass for black.

Collectively, they are known as prayer plants. This is because of the tendency of their otherwise almost horizontal leaves to move into an upright position at night, just like two hands being placed together in prayer.

The most widely grown is *Maranta leuconeura* 'Erythroneura'. Its common name is herringbone plant, due to the bright red veins that emanate from the pale midrib of the leaf. The leaf of *M. leuconeura* 'Massangeana' has an almost black background and pale silver markings along the lid rib and leaf veins. *M. leuconeura* 'Kerchoveana' has perhaps the least spectacular leaf patterning. It is still striking and is commonly known as rabbit tracks or rabbit's foot because of the pairs of dark blotches that are arranged evenly up the centre of the grey-green leaves.

Their colour will only be shown at its best if they are grown in shade in summer. Bright sunlight fades the colours and they will really suffer if placed somewhere that

Maranta leuconeura

receives even a small amount of direct sunlight. Despite this, they need more light in winter. Move them to a brighter spot for the winter but still keep them out of sunlight.

Humidity is important, and they should be misted frequently in summer, particularly in warm weather. Try placing plants in or near a pebble tray or a tray of expanded clay granules. Even in winter an occasional spray of mist will help to keep the plant happy. When watering, use soft, tepid water. If you live in a hard-water area, collect fresh rainwater and use that to water plants.

soil	This plant will grow well if planted into a multi-purpose compost
temp	Grow in hot house conditions or in a conservatory at a minimum of 15°C (59°F)
water & humidity	Water well, sparingly in winter with soft, tepid water. High humidity all year, especially when warm
general care	To propagate, divide plants when re-potting in spring. Give divided plants good humidity when establishing
pests & diseases	Red spider mites are a problem in low humidity. Fading leaf colour is a sign of too much light

Maranta leuconeura 'Kerchoveana'

	SPRING	SUMMER	AUTUMN	WINTER	height (cm)	spread (cm)	leaf colour	
Maranta leuconeura 'Erythroneura'		● ● ●			30	30		Colourful leaves have a velvety texture
M. leuconeura 'Kerchoveana'		● ● ●			30	30		Bold patterning to leaves
M. leuconeura 'Massangeana'		● ● ●			30	30		Leaves have purple undersides

● *flowering*

Medinilla magnifica

Rose grape

Medinilla magnifica, sometimes known as the rose grape, makes an extremely unusual conservatory plant. It has large, glossy dark green leaves with pale, prominent veins. In spring and summer, pendent, dark-pink flower stalks carry clusters of small, pink flowers overhung with large, pink, wing-like bracts.

While this flowerhead could not exactly be described as pretty, it does have a strange beauty of its own and the plant makes an individual contribution to a conservatory plant collection. It is less suitable for a greenhouse unless you are able to provide high temperatures all year.

It will really flower well and look its best if grown in a conservatory. Good warmth year round as well as good levels of filtered

soil	This plant will grow well if planted into a multi-purpose compost
temp	Grow in a hot house or in a conservatory kept at a minimum of 15°C (59°F)
water & humidity	Requires high humidity year round so mist regularly. Water well in summer, but sparingly in winter
general care	Prune, if necessary, straight after flowering. Provide high levels of filtered light and shade from sun
pests & diseases	Scale insects can be a problem. Red spider mite can occur, particularly if high humidity is not maintained

light will ensure a good crop of flowers. Take care to shade plants from the heat of the direct midday sun if possible. Plants kept in dull, cool or dry conditions will most probably be a disappointment. However, the rose grape's main requirement is for a high level of humidity. Try placing the plant's container in a tray of moist expanded clay granules, which will raise the humidity immediately around it. Damp down the floor and benches near the plant regularly, and place it with other humidity loving plants.

Medinilla can also make quite a large plant when grown in the wild, but it should stay smaller, at around 1m (3ft) in height, when grown in a container under glass. If you do need to prune it to keep it to even smaller proportions, do so just after flowering has finished in late summer or early autumn. Take care not to ruin the shape of the plant by pruning too hard.

It is a fairly straightforward plant to propagate from cuttings. Stem cuttings taken in spring or summer can be rooted in a heated propagator.

Mimosa pudica
Sensitive plant

Mimosa pudica goes by the charming common names of sensitive plant and humble plant. These names arise from the way the small leaflets fold into themselves when touched or disturbed. The whole leaf then droops in a self-effacing manner, as if the plant is trying not to be noticed.

Mimosa pudica

After a short while, *M. pudica* leaves unfold again and return to their original shape. This unusual feature makes this a wonderful plant for children to enjoy and appreciate. However, the stems do have spines on them so take care to supervise children when they are near the plant.

Although the leaves alone make Mimosa worth growing, it also has beautiful flowers. These small, fluffy pink balls are produced in summer, along the stems. Although the sensitive plant is actually a perennial, it is best to grow it as an annual from seed each year, and then throw the old plant away in autumn. This way the plant will stay compact and attractive. It is shrubby in habit and usually grows up to about 50cm (20in) in height and spread.

Light is important to Mimosa plants, but they are best if grown in a spot that receives slightly filtered light. They should have shade from direct, midday, summer sun. Throughout the summer it is important to give them high levels of humidity, so place them with other humidity lovers and damp down the greenhouse or conservatory regularly. You could also keep a tray of moist expanded clay granules near the plant or grow them with other plants on a bench full of clay granules. Misting regularly will also help. Although they love humidity, they also need good ventilation, particularly in hot weather.

Watering should be sufficient but not excessive, and these plants will grow best if they are fed occasionally over the

soil	Grows well if planted into a multi-purpose compost with grit and sand incorporated
temp	Grow in a warm greenhouse or in a conservatory kept at a minimum of 13°C (55°F)
water & humidity	Water well and provide high humidity in summer. Plants are usually thrown away in autumn.
general care	Treat as an annual and grow new plants each year from seed sown in a heated propagator in spring
pests & diseases	Red spider mite attack and cause problems for Mimosa plants, particularly if high humidity is not maintained

growing period. Once every fortnight with a liquid fertilizer should be plenty.

Start new plants off in spring in a heated propagator. Prick out into individual pots as soon as plants are large enough. The compost they are potted into should be a mixture of multi-purpose compost, peat and grit, which will provide the well-drained conditions the plant requires. You can also take cuttings from the plant in summer. Again, grow them in a heated propagator to encourage roots to form. If you do want to keep the plant from year to year, cut the plant back fairly hard in winter. Throughout winter, keep watering at a minimum.

Do not confuse *M. pudica* with its relative, *Acacia dealbata*, which is known by the common name mimosa.

Mimosa pudica flowerhead

Monstera deliciosa

Swiss cheese plant

When asked to name a foliage plant, many people would think of Monstera, the Swiss cheese plant. Their beautiful, glossy green leaves, deeply cut and filled with large holes, have made them extremely popular as conservatory and indoor plants. They also grow to an impressive size extremely quickly.

Monsteras originate in the rainforests of Central and South America. They start life in the shade of the forest floor, but as soon as they can find something to climb up they are away, clambering up trees trying to reach higher light levels. However, they are always in shade, and this should be taken as an indication of the conditions they like. Provide light shade in summer and slightly brighter light in winter. If shade is too deep, however, they may fail to develop the holes that give the leaves their distinctive shape.

Monstera deliciosa

They are fairly thirsty plants and will consume lots of water during summer, however, they are also easy to over water.

soil	This plant will grow well if planted into a multi-purpose compost
temp	Grow in hot greenhouse conditions or conservatory at a minimum of 15°C (59°F)
water & humidity	Water well in summer but allow compost to just dry out a little between waterings. Requires average humidity
general care	Monstera plants need strong support. A moss pole will provide a place for aerial roots to attach themselves
pests & diseases	Scale insects and red spider mites. In deep shade, or in cold conditions, leaves can develop without holes

They do have a nifty trick to let you know they have been over watered, though – they start to exude droplets of water from the tips of the leaves. The safest way to water is to allow the compost to almost dry out between waterings.

It is essential to give them some support to clamber up. A thick moss pole is ideal, as they grow by inserting aerial roots into whatever medium they can find. The moss pole should be as sturdy as possible and ideally should be planted deep into the pot at the same time as the plant. Keep the moss pole moist by spraying it occasionally or dribbling water into the top. You could also erect a sturdy trellis or a set of wires to tie the stems onto.

Their size is usually seen as a bonus, but they can become a little overbearing and often end up filling any space made available to them. Mature plants can become a real problem as the tops become heavy and they are difficult to keep upright. It is a good idea to plant them in large, heavy terracotta pots, to help prevent them from becoming top heavy. If they get too large they can be cut back fairly successfully. The plant will re-sprout and any material that has been removed can be used as cuttings.

They are not really suitable for a greenhouse unless you are able to provide high temperatures year round. Instead, use them to provide lush, jungley foliage in a conservatory that is kept at high temperatures all year.

Musa
Banana

If you want your greenhouse or conservatory to have a tropical look then you must buy a banana plant. Their fresh green leaves can grow huge and will provide a wonderfully exotic background for any display of plants.

Musa basjoo

Musa forms a trunk as it grows, and the large, paddle-shaped leaves arch out from the top of this. In fact, this is not a true trunk at all, but is composed of the old bases of the leaves. The older leaves should be cut away from the plant as they age and turn brown, and they will add to the trunk.

Many species produce large, solid and brightly coloured flowers in summer. These often go on to form fruit. These fruits are not usually edible – most ornamental banana fruits have large seeds and the flesh is not tasty – but they are attractive and are often produced in bright colours such as red or green. For edible fruits you would need to grow *Musa acuminata* 'Dwarf Cavendish'. This plant needs high temperatures to flower and fruit successfully.

Banana plants can grow pretty large and may outgrow the average conservatory or greenhouse. However, they constantly throw up suckers that quickly develop into large plants. You can then discard the older larger plants and use the suckers to replace them.

Water freely throughout summer and continue into winter, although not at quite such a high rate. Feed once a month during the growing season. Humidity should be high all year, except during the coldest winter weather. Place trays of expanded clay granules near the plants and keep them constantly moist. Group bananas with other humidity lovers and damp down the greenhouse or conservatory regularly. Good light will help them to grow well, but provide shade from direct midday sun in summer.

Bananas can be planted or put outside in summer, but keep them well-sheltered, as leaves can be damaged by strong winds.

soil	This plant will grow well if it is planted into a multi-purpose compost
temp	Cool or warm house; 7°C (45°F) minimum (*M. acuminata* 'Dwarf Cavendish')
water & humidity	Water well all year, but keep soil a little dryer in winter. Requires high humidity all year
general care	Suckers are thrown up from the side of the plant. Detached, they will quickly grow into large plants
pests & diseases	Occasionally aphids and red spider mites can both attack and cause problems for Musa plants

Musa acuminata 'Dwarf Cavendish'

	SPRING	SUMMER	AUTUMN	WINTER	height (cm)	spread (cm)	flower colour	
Musa acuminata 'Dwarf Cavendish'		● ● ●			300	300		Produces edible fruits if temperatures high enough
M. basjoo		● ● ●			500	400		Elegant shape to leaves
M. coccinea		● ● ●			150	100		An attractive plant of manageable size
M. velutina		● ● ●			150	100		Produces inedible red fruit

● *flowering*

Myrtus
Myrtle

Grow *Myrtus communis*, commonly known as myrtle, to bring the sights and scents of the Mediterranean to cooler climes. Myrtle originates in southern Europe and is among the oldest cultivated plants.

Myrtle is almost hardy and can be grown in gardens in temperate climates. However, unless you live in a particularly mild spot, the plants will not be reliably hardy and will not flower or fruit as well as they do under glass.

Myrtus communis

Although it is not a particularly showy plant, myrtle has an understated charm, and certainly provides value for the space it takes up. Its small, glossy, dark green, evergreen leaves give off a spicy, aromatic scent. The white flowers are produced from spring right through to autumn, and are also beautifully scented. They start off bowl shaped and then open to reveal a mass of stamens. Small flowering sprigs can be cut and will make an aromatic addition to a small bunch of flowers. After

Myrtus communis subsp. *tarentina*

soil	Will grow well if planted into a well-drained multi-purpose compost
temp	Grow in cool greenhouse conditions with a minimum temperature of 4°C (39°F)
water & humidity	Water fairly well in the summer and sparingly in the winter. Requires normal humidity
general care	While small enough, place the plant out of doors during warm spells in summer to help encourage flowering
pests & diseases	Myrtus is easy to grow and does not suffer from any particular problems with pests and diseases

flowering, small back berries are sometimes produced.

As they are almost hardy, they do not need high greenhouse temperatures to grow well and may suffer if the temperature gets too high. They will do well in a greenhouse or conservatory that is kept just above freezing in winter and is left unheated in summer. During warm summer spells it is important to ventilate well to bring the temperature down.

M. communis is quite a large plant for the average conservatory or greenhouse, reaching up to 3m (10ft) in height and spread. Although it can be pruned to keep it down to size, you may consider growing the smaller, but just as attractive *M. communis* subsp. *tarentina*. Myrtles also respond well to being trained in tiers or in a fan against a wall, where their flowers will be well shown off and they will give off their scent without taking up too much space.

M

Conservatory & Greenhouse Plants

	SPRING	SUMMER	AUTUMN	WINTER	height (cm)	spread (cm)	flower colour	
Myrtus communis	● ● ●	● ● ●	● ● ●		300	300		Plant has fragrant leaves and scented flowers
M. communis subsp. *tarentina*	● ● ●	● ● ●	● ● ●		150	150		Compact plant with characteristics of the species

● *flowering*

Narcissus
Daffodil

A pot of flowering daffodils is a wonderful addition to the greenhouse. Many produce a fresh, spring-like scent.

Narcissus cantabricus

Although Narcissi are hardy, there are some that require alpine house conditions in order to flower at their best. These plants are more delicate in appearance than the narcissus plants that are usually grown, and they may need to be sourced from a specialist grower. The reason they need to be grown under cover is that they like to be kept almost completely dry during summer, when the foliage has died down and the plant is dormant. *Narcissus cantabricus* produces its pale, delicate flowers so early in spring that they are often damaged by winter weather when grown outside and are hard to appreciate fully if they were not grown under a little cover.

To create alpine house conditions, you will need a cold greenhouse that is left completely unheated all winter. It should receive as much ventilation as possible, particularly when the weather is warm, and you may need to leave vents and windows open at all times.

Narcissi are usually bought as bulbs in autumn and then potted up in compost. It is

Narcissus cantabricus

soil	Will grow well if planted into a multi-purpose compost with grit incorporated
temp	Grow in cold greenhouse conditions or in an alpine house
water & humidity	Water carefully as bulb starts into growth, increase watering during flowering. Keep dry while dormant
general care	When growth and flower buds appear, turn pot regularly to prevent plant leaning towards the light
pests & diseases	Incorrect forcing can cause problems with non-flowering and damaged flowers. Short lived if too warm

possible to buy bulbs in growth and in flower, although these will be much more expensive. If you are buying bulbs, make sure they are healthy looking and firm. Plant close together in a shallow pot filled with a mixture of compost and grit and cover with compost so that the tips of the bulbs are just below the surface and water in. After this, check occasionally to ensure that the containers have not dried out. It should take around three weeks for flower buds to form. Move the bulbs to a bright but cool spot and enjoy the flowers.

After flowering, bulbs should be fed and watered until the leaves have completely died down. Once the leaves are dead, it is important to keep the bulbs dry. They will start to grow again in early spring, and at this time you should start to gradually increase watering.

	SPRING	SUMMER	AUTUMN	WINTER	height (cm)	spread (cm)	flower colour	
Narcissus cantabricus				● ●	15	10	☐	Tiny outer petals and a large rounded trumpet
N. 'Pipit'	● ●				25	15	☐	Flowers are scented
N. romiexii	●				10	5	☐	Large, rounded trumpet is main feature of flower
N. rupicola	●				15	10	▦	Pretty, bright yellow flowers

● *flowering*

Nelumbo
Lotus

Nelumbo is commonly known as the lotus flower. It is an aquatic plant that grows from and dies back to rhizomes each year.

Nelumbo nucifera

The foliage alone would make this plant worth growing. It is borne on tall stems held above the water and comprises a huge, round leaf, often with a blueish bloom. However, the flowers are really spectacular. They are reminiscent of water lilies but are borne on tall stems, held above the foliage. Plants will flower all summer in shades of white, yellow, cream and pink.

For a plant with such exotic looks and associations, nelumbo does not need much heat. It will be happy in a greenhouse or conservatory that is kept frost free with a minimum temperature of 4°C (39°F) in winter, although *Nelumbo lutea* prefers slightly warmer temperatures and should be kept at a minimum of 7°C (45°F).

To grow these plants successfully you will need to construct an indoor pool.

soil	Should be grown in an aquatic compost in a pool of water
temp	Grow in cool greenhouse conditions with a minimum temperature of 7°C (45°F)
water & humidity	Should be submerged in pool of water throughout growing season. Rhizomes kept moist all year round
general care	Start rhizomes into growth in small amount of water. As growth continues, gradually lower rhizomes into pool
pests & diseases	Whiteflies and red spider mite can attack young growth and cause problems for plants of Nelumbo

Nelumbo should be kept in water all through the growing season. The rhizomes can either be lifted and stored, moist, over the winter or can be left in the pool.

It is possible to grow lotus flowers from seed if you scarify the seeds, give them a little bottom heat and keep them moist, but they may take several years to reach flowering size. Instead, try to buy them as rhizomes. You may have to visit a specialist nursery in order to track them down as they are not widely grown. When you have the rhizomes, start them into growth in a little water in the greenhouse in spring. As the plant starts to grow, move it to the pool, but do not immediately drop it to the bottom of the water. Instead, provide some support so that it is kept near the surface, and gradually move the plant lower and lower into the water as more growth appears.

Nelumbo nucifera 'Mrs Perry D. Slocum'

	SPRING	SUMMER	AUTUMN	WINTER	height (cm)	spread (cm)	flower colour	
Nelumbo nucifera		● ● ●			100	100		Flowers can be double
N. nucifera 'Mrs Perry D. Slocum'		● ● ●			100	100		Petals are yellow at bottom and pink at tip
N. lutea		● ● ●			150	150		Pale flowers held on high flower stalks

● *flowering*

Nepenthes
Pitcher plant

Of the many curiosities that can be grown in a greenhouse or conservatory, the carnivorous plants must be among the most fascinating. Like all plants in this group, Nepenthes has some strange features, but unlike many it grows to an impressive size.

Nepenthes is a carnivorous plant that does not need examining close up to be appreciated.

Nepenthes, often known as pitcher plants, originate in areas with poor soils, and so have developed traps to lure and catch insects. These then decompose and provide them with the nutrients they need to live. In Nepenthes, these traps come in the form of pitchers. They are actually the ends of leaves, modified to create a pitcher shape. Insects are attracted to the scent of nectar produced on the inside of the edge of the pitcher. Once inside, the sides of the pitcher walls are hard to grip

soil	Grow in equal parts peat and sphagnum moss and place crocks in pot for drainage
temp	Grow in hot greenhouse or in a conservatory, minimum temperature of 16°C (61°F)
water & humidity	Water well while actively growing from spring to autumn, and less in winter. Requires high humidity
general care	These are climbing plants, so provide the support of a trellis or wires and tie the stems in regularly
pests & diseases	Mealy bugs and grey mould can cause problems. If pitchers are not forming, light levels are too low

Nepenthes x coccinea

and the insect drops into the well of liquid at the base.

It is essential to recreate the soil in which pitcher plants live in the wild, in order to grow them successfully in the conservatory or greenhouse. A mixture of peat and sphagnum moss makes a good substrate that will be fairly easy to keep moist. Water well while the plant is growing and less in winter, but do not let the compost dry out at any point. You should also feed the plant with a liquid fertilizer over the time it is producing pitchers, normally from spring to autumn.

Nepenthes are climbing plants, so erect a trellis or set of wires for them to climb up. They are also large plants and will need pruning to keep them down to size. Do this in spring. Do not cut the plant down to the ground, but just prune back each stem to about half its length.

	SPRING	SUMMER	AUTUMN	WINTER	height (cm)	spread (cm)	flower colour	
Nepenthes x coccinea	●	● ● ●	●		300	300	▮	Pitchers are mottled dark red
N. mirabilis	●	● ● ●	●		400	400	▮	Pitchers are green with red markings

Nepenthes x coccinea

Conservatory & Greenhouse Plants

● *flowering*

Nephrolepis
Boston fern

The species and cultivars of Nephrolepis are the most beautiful of the ferns. They have gracefully arching bright green fronds and can grow large and impressive. They are available in many different forms and shades.

One of the best known is *Nephrolepis exaltata* 'Bostoniensis', commonly known as the Boston fern. It has long, arching, fronds. *N. exaltata* 'Golden Boston' is similar in shape and size but has pale green or yellow fronds.

Other cultivars can have fronds that are finely divided or crimped.

Because of their shape, they are perfect for growing from a hanging basket, so that their fronds can hang below the container. If you use a wire-framed, moss-lined hanging basket, rather than just suspending a traditional pot, the fronds will burst out through the base.

As ferns go, these are among the easiest to grow, but they still need high humidity and careful watering to ensure they do not dry out. Mist well throughout the growing season and damp down the greenhouse or conservatory regularly. Grow among other ferns and humidity loving plants.

It is important to grow Nephrolepis plants in an acidic compost, so take care to choose ericaceous or lime free when potting on. To help keep the soil conditions acidic you should water with soft water. In hard-water areas you may find it necessary to collect fresh rainwater and use that to water plants.

As with all ferns, low humidity will lead to leaves becoming crispy and brown, and then dying off altogether. However, as the plant ages, some of the older leaves will naturally die back and these should be cut off at the base to encourage new growth. If you have a form with unusually shaped or coloured leaves, look out for any different leaves that emerge. These should be cut back completely or else the plant will completely revert.

soil	Will grow best if planted into a well-drained ericaceous compost
temp	Grow in a warm greenhouse or in a conservatory. Minimum temperature of 10°C (50°F)
water & humidity	Water well in summer and sparingly in winter using soft water and keeping compost moist. High humidity
general care	Will grow best in bright filtered light or in shade. Protect the delicate fronds from direct sunlight
pests & diseases	Scale insects and red spider mite. Fronds will turn brown and die back if the humidity is not high enough

Nephrolepis exaltata 'Bostoniensis'

Conservatory & Greenhouse Plants

	SPRING	SUMMER	AUTUMN	WINTER	height (cm)	spread (cm)	leaf colour	
Nephrolepis exaltata 'Bostoniensis'					150	80		Shape of leaves gives plant a graceful habit
N. exaltata 'Golden Boston'					150	80		Similar plant with pale green leaves

Nerine

Nerine is a beautiful flowering bulb that appears when few other bulbs are flowering. It is at the height of its beauty in autumn, producing its umbels of colourful flowers on the ends of tall stems.

Nerine is a bulb that is often grown out of doors in areas with few frosts, as it is almost hardy. However, the best way to be sure of getting a good show from these bulbs is to grow them under glass. They do not need high temperatures, but will do best in a greenhouse that is kept frost-free. However, they do need a period of dormancy, during which time they should not be watered or fed and should be given fairly cool temperatures. Providing this rest period will help to ensure that plants flower year after year and that they do not burn out too quickly.

The two most widely grown nerines are *Nerine bowdenii* and *N. sarniensis*. *N. bowdenii* is the classic Nerine. It produces large umbels of pink flowers. Each

soil	Will grow best if planted into a well-drained multi-purpose compost
temp	Grow in cool greenhouse conditions at a minimum temperature of 4°C (39°F)
water & humidity	Water well when first planted. Keep *N. bowdenii* dry through winter and *N. sarniensis* during summer
general care	Nerines will flower best when the bulbs are congested in the pot, so only re-pot every five years or so
pests & diseases	Aphids and mealy bugs are among the pests that can occasionally attack and cause problems for Nerine

Nerine bowdenii

flower is held on the end of a short stem attached to the top of the main flower stem, and the pink petals are reflexed and wavy-edged. Each flower looks like a tiny lily flower. This plant flowers in autumn and should be rested from the end of flowering until early spring, when watering should begin again.

N. sarniensis is commonly known as the Guernsey Lily, because it has become naturalized on Guernsey. Its head of flowers is far more compact than that of *N. bowdenii* and the colouring is orange or red. Each flower has a set of long, straight stamens that give the flowers extra impact. This plant will flower in early autumn. It should be watered carefully all winter until the end of spring, when watering should stop completely. Towards the end of summer water plants well and then keep watering throughout flowering.

	SPRING	SUMMER	AUTUMN	WINTER	height (cm)	spread (cm)	flower colour	
Nerine bowdenii			● ● ●		45	10		Wavy pink reflexed petals
N. sarniensis			● ●		45	10		Compact brightly coloured flower heads

● *flowering*

Conservatory & Greenhouse Plants

N

Nerium oleander

Oleander

Nerium oleander is the Mediterranean shrub that is more commonly known as oleander. It is a large evergreen shrub that produces its single or double pink flowers throughout spring and summer and into autumn.

Nerium oleander

As oleanders grow outside in Mediterranean winters, it is not necessary to provide them with particularly high temperatures in the greenhouse or conservatory. However, they will benefit from being kept frost free, and will thrive in a situation where the temperature does not drop below 4°C (39°F). They do need plenty of light and should be grown in a spot where they will receive full sunlight for most of the day. In summer they will appreciate good ventilation when the weather is warm. You may even choose to move the plant out of doors during the summer months. Plants will be happy with this treatment and it will free up space inside the conservatory.

Although oleanders can be watered well and fed once every fortnight when actively growing in summer, it is important to reduce watering and to stop feeding in autumn and then to keep plants almost completely dry throughout winter. This allows them to have a proper period of dormancy, which will help them to last well and flower year after year.

You can grow oleander in a conservatory or greenhouse border. However, you may find it better to contain the roots in a large pot as it can grow too large. Potted plants are unlikely to grow beyond 2m (6½ft) in height and spread. You can also keep oleander down to size by pruning in autumn, once flowering has finished. Do not cut the plant right down to the ground, but instead, cut it back to about half its size. This will encourage flowering shoots to form the following year. As the plant is putting on growth in spring, pinch out the tips occasionally to encourage it to branch low down and bush out. This will make the plant a much better shape. You may need to stop this in summer as flowers start to form on the ends of the shoots, or carefully select non-flowering shoots to pinch out.

Take care when handling and pruning oleanders to move all prunings out of the reach of children and pets. All parts of the plant, and in particular the flowers, are poisonous. It may not be sensible to grow this plant if you have small children.

soil	Will grow best if planted into a well-drained multi-purpose compost
temp	Grow in cool greenhouse conditions at a minimum temperature of 4°C (39°F)
water & humidity	Water fairly well in summer, less in autumn and then sparingly during winter. Requires average humidity
general care	This large shrub can be kept down to size by cutting back all newer growth at the beginning of autumn
pests & diseases	Mealy bugs, scale insects and red spider mites can all attack and cause problems for oleanders

Nerium oleander

Nymphaea
Water lily

The hardy species and cultivars of Nymphaea, commonly known as water lilies, are widely grown out of doors in temperate areas. You may then question the need to provide space for them in the greenhouse or conservatory.

The reason for growing them under glass, however, is that there are a number of beautiful and exotic water lilies that are well worth growing and can only be grown with protection in a warm pool.

Among the most prized of these are the blue water lilies, as there are no hardy water lily plants that bear flowers of this colour. These are not murky blues either, but crisp brilliant blues. Another benefit of growing water lilies in an indoor pool is that it opens up a range of night-blooming plants. There are very few hardy night-blooming water lilies, but many of the tender plants open

soil	Best if planted into aquatic compost and submerged in water at all times
temp	Grow in warm greenhouse conditions at a minimum temperature of 10°C (50°F)
water & humidity	Submerge plants in water at all times throughout the year, as long as temperature is maintained
general care	Take care when first putting plants in water to lower them to the bottom in a series of stages
pests & diseases	Water-lily aphids are among some of the pests that can attack and cause problems for Nymphaea plants

Nymphaea 'Perry's Pink'

their flowers at night and close them during the day. These are also often beautifully scented, as they are in the white flowered *Nymphaea* 'Wood's White Knight'. Because of these traits, this plant would make a magical addition to a conservatory that is used for entertaining in the evening.

They do need fairly high temperatures,

and you must be sure to provide a pool of water that is kept at a minimum winter temperature of 10°C (50°F) and a minimum summer temperature of 21°C (70°F). They should be planted in spring, when they are just starting into growth. Plant them into baskets of aquatic compost and place a heavy mulch of stones, grit or pebbles on the surface of the pot, to prevent the compost from floating away. It is essential to lower them into the pool in stages. Small plants dropped to the bottom of the pool can struggle to capture enough daylight to grow and may simply die. Provide a platform of bricks and place the plant on top of this so that the leaves just reach the surface. As the plant grows you can gradually lower it further into the pool until it is on the bottom.

	SPRING	SUMMER	AUTUMN	WINTER	height (cm)	spread (cm)	flower colour	
Nymphaea capensis		● ● ●			10	200		Clear blue flowers with a yellow centre
N. 'General Pershing'		● ● ●			10	150		Bears scented pink flowers
N. mexicana		● ● ●			10	250		Variably coloured star-shaped flowers
N. 'Perry's Pink'		● ● ●			10	250		Light pink blooms
N. 'Wood's White Knight'		● ● ●			10	250		Scented flowers open at night

Conservatory & Greenhouse Plants

N

● *flowering*

Paphiopedilum
Slipper orchid

Plants in the genus Paphiopedilum are better known under their common name of the slipper orchid. They are so called because of the unusual shape of the lower petals, which have fused into a pouch, which sometimes resemble a slipper.

These bizarre flowers, which also have an enlarged upper petal and two wing-like petals at the side of the flower, are usually borne singly, on dark stems that help to show them off. The colour range is also unusual, dominated as it is by greens, browns and dark purples. They are grown for their curiosity value, but they are also strangely attractive.

Paphiopedilum insigne is one of the easier to grow as it does not require temperatures as high as some, although it will still require a minimum of 10°C (50°F). It has particularly bizarre flowers in green yellow and a shade of brownish purple. *P. fairreanum* has a striking pattern of deep purple-red veins on a white background on its petals and paler veins on its pouch. *P.* Maudiae has striped petals.

To successfully grow slipper orchids, you will need to pot them into a specially prepared orchid compost. This should include bark chippings and sphagnum moss to allow water to drain freely. It must have an open texture or roots can start to rot. In summer, provide plenty of bright, filtered light and high humidity. It is better to avoid misting the leaves and instead to provide a pebble tray or a tray filled with moist expanded clay granules. You should also place them near other humidity-loving plants and damp down the greenhouse or conservatory regularly. Water well in summer and feed with a quarter-strength liquid feed every few weeks. In winter allow the plant into full light and keep watering so that the compost never completely dries out.

soil	Best in an open orchid compost that includes bark chips and sphagnum moss
temp	Grow in warm greenhouse conditions at a minimum temperature of 10°C (50°F)
water & humidity	Water well in summer and sparingly in winter but do not allow the compost to dry out. Requires high humidity
general care	Grow plants in good filtered light in summer but allow as much light as is available during winter
pests & diseases	Mealy bug, scale insect and aphid are among the pests that can sometimes attack and cause problems

Paphiopedilum Maudiae

	SPRING	SUMMER	AUTUMN	WINTER	height (cm)	spread (cm)	flower colour	
Paphiopedilum fairrieanum			● ● ●		15	15		Purple veins cover parts of the flowers
P. insigne	● ● ●		● ● ●	● ● ●	15	25		Flowers are patterned with spots
P. Maudiae	● ● ●	● ● ●			30	15		Green and white stripes to flowers

● *flowering*

Conservatory & Greenhouse Plants

P

Passiflora
Passion flower

Passiflora plants, commonly known as passion flowers, can be grown out of doors. However, there are many tender species and cultivars that need the protection of a greenhouse or conservatory to grow well.

The tender species also happen to be the choicest of the bunch and their flowers make the hardier plants pale in comparison.

Passion flowers are grown for their beautiful flowers. They comprise an open circle of petals inside which sit a ring of often brightly coloured filaments, that may blend in or contrast with the colour of the petals. The stamens at the centre of the flower are often brightly and contrastingly coloured themselves, and are as much a feature of the flower as the petals. Fruits follow the flowers, and these are edible, but they are only really worth eating if you grow *Passiflora edulis*.

The flowers come in shades of white, red, orange-red, pink and, most commonly, purple. They flower throughout summer. The single coloured flowers, such as *P. antioquensis* in a deep pinkish-red, are just as beautiful as the more complex

soil	Best in multi-purpose compost, planted into a greenhouse or conservatory
temp	Grow in warm greenhouse conditions at a minimum temperature of 13°C (55°F)
water & humidity	Water well during growth from spring to autumn and sparingly in winter. Requires average humidity
general care	Prune in late winter before growth begins to keep plants down to size. Cut back all stems by about half
pests & diseases	Red spider mite, aphids, scale insects and cucumber mosaic virus can all cause problems for Passiflora

flowers. *P. racemosa* is a flower in which the filament is fairly reduced and so the bright, pillar-box red flower looks fairly simple and elegant. Among the more complicated flowers are those of *P. quadrangularis*, which have a huge ring of purple and white striped filaments, which are wavy at the ends.

These are large plants and will be happiest grown in a large container. They can also be grown in a greenhouse or conservatory border. Either way, top-dress them regularly in spring with fresh compost. They should be cut back in late winter to keep them down to a manageable size. Take all of the stems back to half their length, or more if necessary. They will enjoy good light, but should be kept protected from the heat of the midday sun.

Passiflora quadrangularis

	SPRING	SUMMER	AUTUMN	WINTER	height (cm)	spread (cm)	flower colour	
Passiflora antioquensis		● ● ●			400	100	■	Large, simple, brilliantly coloured flowers
P. edulis		● ● ●			500	200	□	Tasty edible fruit produced
P. quadrangularis		● ● ●			1000	300	▮	Prominent filaments are the main feature of the flower
P. racemosa		● ● ●			400	100	■	Striking flowers in clear, bright red
P. 'Star of Bristol'		● ● ●			400	100	■	Purple flowers followed by orange fruit

● *flowering*

Pelargonium
Geranium

Pelargoniums, known as geraniums, are so easy to grow and make extremely good conservatory and greenhouse plants. There is huge variation in the colours of the flowers and form of their flowers and foliage. Many will even flower all year round.

The classic pelargoniums are those in the zonal group. The Regal and Angel pelargoniums make even better greenhouse and conservatory plants. Both groups form a good, bushy shape and have large, showy, colourful flowers. The ivy-leaved pelargoniums are more elegant. They have solid, waxy leaves and a trailing habit, making them good for hanging baskets. They also have attractive, colourful flowers. The scented pelargoniums, known as scented geraniums, emit delicious rose, lemon or even peppermint smells when the leaves are crushed, brushed past or even when they are watered. Their flowers are pretty, but they are small and insignificant in comparison with the bright colours and blousy shapes of the flowering geraniums. Many people prefer their subtlety, even without the added bonus of the leaves.

The main flowering time for pelargoniums is late spring to mid-summer. During this time they can be

Pelargonium 'Ann Hoysted'

watered well, but it is important to allow the compost to almost dry out between waterings. It is easy to over water pelargoniums and this can cause rots and other problems. In summer, keep plants well ventilated. They will suffer in high levels of humidity. Water on the leaves can lead to rots and moulds developing.

In autumn as temperatures fall, flowering will decrease and the plant can be dried out and kept almost dry for winter. Cut the plant back at this time by at least half to encourage fresh growth in spring. In warm environments, pelargoniums can keep flowering throughout winter. To encourage this, keep plants in a warm, light place and keep watering, but less than in summer.

Pelargonium 'Attar of Roses'

soil	Will grow best if planted into a well-drained multi-purpose compost
temp	Grow in cool greenhouse conditions at a minimum temperature of 4°C (39°F)
water & humidity	In summer water well, allow to dry out in between waterings. Low humidity. Keep almost dry in winter
general care	Should be cut back in spring and have their growing tips regularly pinched out to encourage bushiness
pests & diseases	Vine weevils, aphids, whiteflies, thrips, botrytis and black leg. Over-watering leads to fungal problems

Pelargonium 'L'Élegante'

	SPRING	SUMMER	AUTUMN	WINTER	height (cm)	spread (cm)	flower colour
Pelargonium 'Ann Hoysted'	●	● ● ●			45	25	Deep red flowered regal pelargonium
P. 'Apple Blossom Rosebud'	●	● ● ●			40	25	Clusters of pink to white flowers – zonal pelargonium
P. 'Attar of Roses'		● ● ●			60	30	Rose scented foliage
P. 'L'Élegante'	● ●	● ● ●			25	20	Variegated ivy-leaved pelargonium
P. 'Tip Top Duet'	●	● ● ●			40	20	Angel pelargonium

● *flowering*

Phalaenopsis
Moth orchid

Phalaenopsis is the most graceful and elegant of the orchids. It bears single, arching flower spikes dotted with flowers. It is sometimes known as the moth orchid, for the open, rounded shape of the flowers.

On some Phalaenopsis plants the flowers are large and sparse, while on other plants the flower spikes are covered in small blooms.

Phalaenopsis does need a fair amount of heat if it is to do well and flower regularly, and so it is only really suitable if you plan to keep a really warm greenhouse or conservatory. Ideally, they should have hot house conditions. Place plants in a place where they will receive lots of bright, filtered light. They should be watered freely while in growth in summer, and fed every three weeks or so with a quarter-strength liquid feed. Humidity should be high, and you should mist plants at least once a day or damp down the greenhouse or conservatory on at least a daily basis. In winter, keep plants in full light and water just enough to keep the compost moist.

soil	Will grow best if planted into a bark-containing epiphytic orchid compost
temp	Grow in hot house conditions at a minimum temperature of 18°C (64°F)
water & humidity	In the growing season water well. Water sparingly in winter. Requires high humidity all year round
general care	It is important to remove dead flowers regularly in order to encourage more flower buds to form
pests & diseases	Aphids and mealy bugs can cause problems. Red spider mite is a problem, particularly in low humidity

These types of orchids are epiphytic, meaning that in the wild they grow in the cracks between branches high up in the canopies of trees. Because of this they will really suffer – and their roots may rot – if they are planted into a close-textured compost. Their compost should be a chunky, free-draining one and should contain a large amount of bark chippings to mirror the conditions they encounter in the wild.

When flowering spikes are formed, they will often last for at least two months. After they have finally faded, remove them to encourage even more flowers to form.

Propagation is tricky because, unlike most other orchids, they cannot be divided. It is possible to root cuttings if they are taken in spring and given a little bottom heat.

Phalaenopsis amabilis 'Doris'

	SPRING	SUMMER	AUTUMN	WINTER	height (cm)	spread (cm)	flower colour	
Phalaenopsis amabilis	●		●●●	●●●	30	30		Graceful white flowers
P. equestris	●●●	●●●		●●	20	20		Produces small, pink flowers
P. stuartiana	●		●●●	●●●	60	30		Marking on lower petals

● *flowering*

Philodendron

Philodendrons are handsome foliage plants that are available in a number of different forms. They are extremely tolerant of shady conditions, and make imposing specimen plants for any dark corners. All have large, glossy, impressive leaves.

Philodendron erubescens

Many philodendrons are climbers. *Philodendron scandens* is perhaps the best known of these. Its leaves are heart-shaped and glossy and have given it the common name of sweetheart plant. Another good climbing type is *P. bipennifolium*. It is known as the fiddle leaf due to its unusual shaped leaves, which are arrow shaped, with one particularly prominent lobe. Many Philodendron have young leaves and stems that are flushed with red or bronze, adding to the interest provided by the foliage. *P. erubescens* 'Imperial Red' has particularly colourful leaves, flushed deep red.

The other main type of Philodendron are those with a shrubby habit. *P. bipinnatifidum* has large, deeply lobed leaves with a wavy margin. They tend to spread their handsome leaves outwards, so need to be placed in a spot where they have plenty of space and will not be too regularly brushed by passing people.

The main requirements

Philodendron needs to keep it healthy are shade, humidity and warmth. Keep in a shady spot that receives no direct sunlight and mist or damp down around the plants regularly, particularly in warm weather. Grow climbing plants up a sturdy moss pole kept moist by regular misting or by dribbling water into the top. This will raise the humidity further. Because the leaves are glossy, wash them regularly and polish them with leaf wipes, otherwise they will start to look dusty and dull, and growth will be slowed down.

When watering, use soft, tepid water. In hard-water areas, collect rainwater and use it while it is still fresh. In soft water areas you should be able to use tap water, but leave it to stand for a while so that it reaches room temperature before you use it on the plant.

Generally, these are large plants that grow quickly and you may find that it is necessary to pot them on every year. If a plant is growing too large, prune it back in winter.

Philodendron bipinnatifidum

soil	This plant will grow well if planted into a multi-purpose compost
temp	Grow in warm greenhouse conditions with a minimum temperature of 13°C (55°F)
water & humidity	Water well in summer, keep just moist in winter. Average to high humidity. Raise humidity in warm weather
general care	Climbing types require a sturdy moss pole, kept moist throughout summer, for the aerial roots to grow into
pests & diseases	Scale insects and red spider mite. Leaves turning pale indicate that plant is receiving too much light

	SPRING	SUMMER	AUTUMN	WINTER	height (cm)	spread (cm)	leaf colour	
Philodendron angutisectum		● ● ●			400	150		Particularly vigorous growing plant
P. bipennifolium		● ● ●			400	150		Prominent leaf lobes give plant a distinctive look
P. bipinnatifidum		● ● ●			400	400		Plant has deeply lobed leaves
P. erubescens		● ● ●			300	100		Red stalk and leaf backs
P. erubescens 'Imperial Red'		● ● ●			300	100		Red tinted leaves
P. scandens		● ● ●			300	100		Plant has heart shaped leaves

● *flowering*

Conservatory & Greenhouse Plants

Phoenix
Date palm

Phoenix is a beautifully shaped palm. Out of doors, in warm climates, some date palms can grow up to 30m (100ft) in height. However, when these same plants are young, they make unusual and attractive indoor plants.

Phoenix canariensis is known as the Canary Island date palm. In the wild or in warm climates it will grow up to 15m (49ft) in height, but it will not grow nearly this large in a container. Canary Island date palms have large, arching leaves from which grow many long, pointed leaflets. As the plant grows the lower leaves die away. This is part of the plant's natural growth pattern and should not be taken as a sign of disease. Dead leaves should be cut back to their base – they will become part of the plant's stocky trunk. The Canary Island date palm should be kept as a conservatory or greenhouse plant until it is too large, when

soil	This plant will grow well if planted into a multi-purpose compost
temp	Grow in warm greenhouse conditions with a minimum temperature of 10°C (50°F)
water & humidity	Water well in summer and sparingly in winter. Average humidity for *P. canariensis*, high for *P. roebelinii*
general care	Propagate from the suckers produced around the base of the plant. These should be potted up in spring
pests & diseases	Scale insects and red spider mite can cause problems. Lower leaves turn yellow and brown. Remove them

Phoenix canariensis

it should be discarded and replaced. Suckers are regularly produced at the base of the plant and these can be separated off as soon as they are large enough and grown on to become young replacement plants.

P. roebelinii is known as the miniature date palm as it grows to just 2m (6½ft) in height in its native habitat. It grows extremely slowly so is a better size for a conservatory or greenhouse. It does, however, require higher humidity than *P. canariensis*, and it should be misted regularly and grown in an area that is frequently damped down.

Apart from the humidity requirement, care of Phoenix plants is fairly straightforward. However, they will grow best in a good, bright spot and will even tolerate a little direct sunlight, although they should be shaded from midday sun at the height of summer.

	SPRING	SUMMER	AUTUMN	WINTER	height (cm)	spread (cm)	leaf colour	
Phoenix canariensis		● ● ●			600	200		Useful plants while still young
P. roebelinii		● ● ●			200	200		Small growing plant that stays compact

● *flowering*

Conservatory & Greenhouse Plants

P

Platycerium bifurcatum

Common staghorn fern

Ferns make a great addition as background greenery to a conservatory or glasshouse that is kept at a high humidity, but few command attention as much as Platycerium, the staghorn fern.

Platycerium bifurcatum is known as the common staghorn fern and it is the most widely grown of the genus. It is an epiphytic fern, which means that it grows in small cracks in trees or sits in the points where branches meet trucks. Because of this it has a small root system and does like an extremely well-drained compost. It is best grown with a small portion of this compost wrapped around the root. Strap the whole plant to a piece of bark or driftwood or grow in a hanging basket.

The plant produces two types of fronds. One is produced at the base of the plant and is sterile and rounded. It gradually grows around whatever it has been strapped too, helping to support the whole plant. In the wild, the pouch shape formed by these fronds acts as a vessel for collecting water and vegetable matter such as falling leaves. These leaves gradually rot down and provide the plant with nutrients that it would struggle to get otherwise in its high perch. The infertile fronds are gradually replaced by new fronds and the plant may build up a number

soil	Grow in a mixture of leaf mould, loam and sphagnum moss
temp	Grow in cool greenhouse conditions with a minimum temperature of 5°C (41°F)
water & humidity	Water well in summer by wetting the root ball, and sparingly in winter. High humidity in summer
general care	The small root should be wrapped in compost and strapped to a piece of bark or into a hanging basket
pests & diseases	Scale insects can occur and can get a hold as they are hard to spot due to the overlapping fronds

of layers of dead fronds. The other type of fronds are fertile and silvery in appearance and are produced from the centre of the plant.

Water is important to all ferns and Platycerium will need lots of it during summer when it is actively growing. It can be best to water the plant from below by soaking the rootball. Feed it occasionally during summer by mixing liquid feed into its usual water and soaking the root with it. High humidity is essential and plants should be misted daily throughout spring and summer. Grow these plants near other ferns and humidity-loving plants, and damp down the area around them regularly, particularly in warm weather.

The fertile fronds will produce spores occasionally and these can be used for propagation. However, you will need to provide high levels of constant warmth and humidity for them to germinate and thrive. It can be easier to propagate from plantlets. These are produced occasionally from the base of the plant and should be carefully teased away from the main plant and potted up in fresh compost.

Platycerium bifurcatum

P

Conservatory & Greenhouse Plants

Plumeria
Frangipani

Plumeria is widely known as the frangipani or the West Indian jasmine. It is an extremely elegant plant that has glossy leaves and beautiful flowers. It is often grown for its beautiful scent.

Plumeria rubra f. *acutifolia*

The flowers of frangipani have an unusual makeup. From afar they look like any other flower, but up close the petals overlap each other slightly on one side of each petal, so that the whole flower has a spiral shape to it and looks as if it has been created by an expert in origami. Each petal is pleasingly curved outwards. *Plumeria rubra* produces its flowers in a pretty deep pink, while *P. rubra* f. *acutifolia* has white petals with a yellow stain at the centre. The scent of both plants is particularly good, and the flowers retain their scent long after they have faded.

They like warmth so will need to be grown in warm greenhouse conditions or in a conservatory that is heated well throughout the year. They can grow quite large in the wild, but will not grow nearly so big if kept contained in a pot. Do not plant out directly into the greenhouse or conservatory border unless you have lots of space.

If plants do start to grow too large for their allotted space, they can be pruned. This should be carried out immediately after flowering. Do not cut the plant back hard but remove a few of the larger stems each year and shorten any that are growing too long. *P. rubra* f. *acutifolia* is a more compact plant and so will be easier to keep down to a manageable size.

Place frangipani plants where they will receive high levels of light, but provide some shade from the midday sun. Humidity is particularly important during flowering, when they should be misted daily.

soil	This plant will grow well if planted into a multi-purpose compost
temp	Grow in warm greenhouse conditions with a minimum temperature of 13°C (55°F)
water & humidity	Water well in summer, sparingly in winter. High humidity is needed only when flowering
general care	Generally easy to maintain. Grow these plants in a container to keep them down to a manageable size
pests & diseases	Scale insects, mealy bug and red spider mites can all occur and cause problems for Plumeria plants

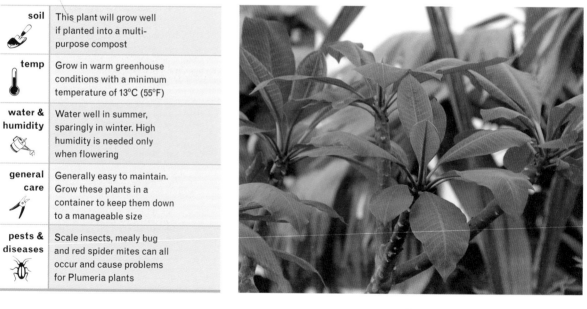

Plumeria rubra f. *acutifolia*

	SPRING	SUMMER	AUTUMN	WINTER	height (cm)	spread (cm)	flower colour	
Plumeria rubra		● ● ●	● ●		500	300	▦	Deep pink flowers with delicious scent
P. rubra f. *acutifolia*		● ●	● ●		350	150	▢	More compact, white-flowered plant

● *flowering*

P

Primula
Primrose

Primulas are compact plants that produce pretty flowers of various colours in winter or spring. There are two main types that can be grown in greenhouses and conservatories, and these should be treated in different ways.

Primula malacoides

Primula obconica 'Gigantea'

soil	Use multi-purpose compost (add grit and leaf mould for alpine types)
temp	Cool greenhouse conditions. Minimum temperature 7°C (45°F); cold house for alpines
water & humidity	Water well in summer, sparingly in winter. Protect alpines from wet in winter and do not wet their foliage
general care	Primulas can be grown from seed or can be propagated by division after they have finished flowering
pests & diseases	Red spider mites, aphids, botrytis and vine weevil can all attack and cause problems for primulas

Purple-flowered *Primula malacoides*, *P. obconica*, with big pink and purple flowers and *P. sinensis*, with delicate, fringed flowers can all be treated almost as houseplants. They are happy in cool greenhouse conditions and should be kept cool during flowering. Site in bright filtered light conditions. Water well during the growing season, and mist and damp down regularly when temperatures are high. They benefit from spending a long spell in late spring and summer outside, where they should be placed in a shady spot and kept well watered. Bring them in before any frosts in autumn. If they are kept indoors over this time, provide good ventilation to keep them cool.

P. allionii and P. sonchifolia are alpines and need different treatment. They should ideally be grown in an alpine house and planted into a sharply drained compost that has been combined with leaf mould. This is a greenhouse that is kept completely unheated throughout the year and may even be ventilated throughout winter. A fan may also be used to keep air moving, particularly in summer. The main purpose of the greenhouse is to protect these plants from winter wet, which would rot their roots. Water fairly well throughout the growing season, but keep almost dry throughout winter. Take care when watering not to wet the foliage, as this can lead to rots and moulds developing. Ventilate well all year round, especially in warm weather, when the plants may need to be placed outdoors in a cool shady spot.

Primula sinensis (top and below)

	SPRING	SUMMER	AUTUMN	WINTER	height (cm)	spread (cm)	flower colour	
Primula allionii	● ● ●			●	10	20		Alpine with pink to purple flowers with a white centre
P. malacoides	● ● ●			● ● ●	40	20		Frilled edges to petals
P. obconica	● ● ●			● ● ●	30	25		Large flowers available in many colours
P. sinensis	●			● ● ●	20	20		Flowers have wavy edges
P. sonchifolia	● ● ●				5	30		Small, spreading alpine plant

● *flowering*

Protea cynaroides
King protea

For just about the most exotic and interesting flowers it is possible to grow in a greenhouse or conservatory, choose Proteas. These are South African plants with truly magnificent blooms.

The flowerheads of the King protea, *Protea cynaroides*, grow up to 13cm (5in) across. These are the best known of the Proteas and the most widely grown, although there are many more that are worth trying. King proteas have flat or slightly pointed centres made up of many small, tubular flowers. Around the outside of this is a ring of pointed pink bracts. Considering the flowers they produce are so impressive, Proteas need very little heat. They will grow at their best in a glasshouse that is kept just frost-free. They really need the protection of a glasshouse or conservatory to keep the winter wet off them and to protect from harder frosts.

As they originate in scrubland in South Africa they are not great moisture lovers. In fact, they will need a well-drained soil that has plenty of horticultural grit mixed into it, as well as some peat, which will make the compost slightly acidic. Proteas should be watered only sparingly and kept fairly dry, even during spring and summer. However, if temperatures rise in summer, this is the time to give them a really good drink.

Feed them only occasionally, using a liquid fertilizer at half its recommended

soil	For this plant use a loam-based compost and add peat and grit
temp	Requires cool greenhouse conditions with a minimum temperature of 4°C (39°F)
water & humidity	Water carefully in the growing season, sparingly in winter. Proteas require low levels of humidity
general care	Move plants out of doors in summer. Make sure they are moved back indoors before frost threatens
pests & diseases	Magnesium deficiency due to poor feeding manifests itself by a yellowing of the leaves

strength. Proteas can occasionally suffer from magnesium deficiency and this manifests itself in a yellowing of the leaves. It can be corrected by applying a fertiliser that contains magnesium and other trace elements.

Proteas can be grown from seed, if the seed is sown in a heated propagator. Remove the tips of young plants as they grow, repeating this every time they put on about 30cm (12in) of growth. This will encourage the plants to branch out and keep a good, bushy shape.

New plants are likely to flower in their third year from seed. The flowers are produced in late spring or summer and will be more intense in colour the cooler the conditions in which they are kept.

They make striking and long-lasting cut flowers. They will last in a vase of water for at least two weeks if the water is changed regularly and the bottoms of the stems are occasionally re-cut. It is also possible to dry them. Wait until the flower is completely open and then hang it upside down in a cool, dry place for about three weeks.

Protea cynaroides

Rebutia

Rebutia species are popular for their compact size and a real ease of flowering. Many will flower after their first year from seed. They readily produce offsets, and therefore spread out and quickly fill up a pot.

They are rewarding, neat and easy to care for cacti and this makes them good plants to try if you have never grown cacti before.

Rebutia fiebrigii is covered in small white spines that form a white haze over the whole plant, giving them a fluffy appearance and making the surface of the stems quite hard to see. It produces a bright orange flower in early summer. *R. minuscula* is smaller and its pink-purple flowers are huge in relation to the diminutive size of the plant. *R. pygmaea* is even smaller again, and has a quirky shape. It has slightly cylindrical stems, rather than the usual round stems, and it produces bright pink flowers in summer.

All Rebutia plants need to be kept in full light, and a spot that receives direct sunlight all year round will suit them well. Unusually for cacti, they do appreciate a little humidity, so in warm summer weather you should take care to mist them occasionally and to water them regularly. In winter they should be kept almost

soil	Will grow best in a free-draining succulent compost with plenty of grit
temp	Requires cool greenhouse conditions with a minimum temperature of 4°C (39°F)
water & humidity	Water this plant carefully in the growing season and sparingly in winter. Needs low humidity
general care	Propagation is particularly easy with rebutias, as offsets are freely formed. Remove them and pot on
pests & diseases	Mealy bugs and red spider mites can attack. Over-watering can lead to moulds and rotting of stems

completely dry. They also prefer to be fairly cool during this time.

They are fairly short-lived plants, but propagation is easy as offsets are freely produced and can easily be removed at re-potting time in spring. Pot each offset up into a shallow pot with good drainage holes, using a standard cactus compost.

Watch out for mealy bugs, which can attack the stems. Other problems are usually associated with over watering, particularly in winter. Rots can form on the stems if the compost is not allowed to dry out for long enough between waterings.

Rebutia fiebrigii

	SPRING	SUMMER	AUTUMN	WINTER	height (cm)	spread (cm)	flower colour	
Rebutia fiebrigii		● ● ●			10	15		Particularly free-flowering species
R. miniscula		● ● ● ● ● ●			5	12		Compact plant with big flowers
P. obconica		● ● ●			4	8		Unusual cylindrical stems

● flowering

Rhododendron simsii

Azalea

Rhododendrons that are grown as indoor and conservatory plants are commonly known as Azaleas. They are plants that bring an exotic touch to the home. The large, papery flowers evoke the Far East, from where they originate.

Most of the plants are in shades of white, pink and red, but there are also other colours including orange and yellow available.

Azaleas flower in winter and spring, and so are good plants for a mid-winter display or for generally brightening up a conservatory or greenhouse during the dull winter months. They are not too difficult to look after, and are fairly easy to encourage back into flower each year.

The best place to keep them while in flower is in a fairly cool spot with good light. Azaleas are not far from being hardy, so they will really not appreciate high temperatures. They should be kept in a well-ventilated spot with a moderate atmosphere and the leaves should be misted regularly, particularly when the plant is in flower. In a warm conservatory or greenhouse with little ventilation, flower buds can often drop before they have opened, and open flowers will be short lived.

Azaleas are lime-haters, and this means that they must be planted out into lime-free soil such as ericaceous compost. This can be bought in garden centres and in many indoor plant departments. It should also be used for every re-potting and top-dressing or the plant will start to suffer.

Caring for lime-haters also means taking care with watering. Hard water contains lime and so regular watering with hard water will eventually damage the plant. Use soft water as often as possible. In hard-water areas, collect rainwater and use it to water plants while it is still fresh. Try to avoid using water from water buts, as this often sits around for a long time and can harbour moulds or diseases that will be harmful to an indoor plant. Azaleas need a lot of water, particularly while flowering when they should be kept almost wet for most of the time.

After flowering is over, trim the plant back and re-pot before placing outside or sinking into a border for the summer. Regular feeding and watering outdoors over summer will give the plant a chance to grow good flowering shoots for the following winter. In autumn, bring into the conservatory or greenhouse and reduce watering to encourage new bud formation.

soil	Requires a lime-free compost such as ericaceous compost to grow at its best
temp	Requires cool greenhouse conditions with a minimum temperature of 7°C (45°F)
water & humidity	Water well, during flowering and sparingly for the rest of year. High humidity while flowering
general care	Keep this plant in bright, filtered light and apply a liquid feed once a month when in growth
pests & diseases	Vine weevil, aphids and scale insects. Yellowing of leaves occurs if not planted in lime-free compost

Rhododendron simsii

Conservatory & Greenhouse Plants

Rhodohypoxis

Rhodohypoxis is an alpine plant that originates in South Africa. It produces brightly coloured star-shaped flowers throughout summer.

Because of its place of origin, Rhodohypoxis is not quite as hardy as some alpine plants, but it should still grow well in an alpine house. This is a greenhouse that is kept completely unheated throughout the year. Normally, alpines thrive in these alpine houses because they are protected from winter rains, which would otherwise rot their stems and roots. Rhodohypoxis appreciates being kept dry in winter, but also enjoys the slight protection an alpine house gives it against the worst of winter frosts.

Alpine houses must be well ventilated at all times of the year, even in the depths of winter. It is also important for them to stay fairly cool in summer, and so some people fit fans in their alpine houses, which help to move the air around on warm, summer days. It is important to discourage any dampness in winter, so watch out for condensation and leaks.

The most commonly grown is *Rhodohypoxis baurii*. This has lovely large

soil	Requires a lime-free compost with added grit for good drainage
temp	Requires cool greenhouse conditions with a minimum temperature of 4°C (39°F)
water & humidity	Water well, using soft water, during the growing season and keep almost dry in winter. Low humidity
general care	Requires good ventilation. To propagate, divide plants in autumn and re-pot in fresh compost
pests & diseases	Red spider mite and thrips can attack. Will suffer from rotting stems if watered too often in winter

flowers in shades between dark and light pink. Most of the other plants of this genera that are grown are cultivars of this species. They have flowers in pink, red, purple or white.

They need a slightly peaty soil, or can be grown in an ericaceous soil as they are lime-haters and will suffer if planted into any compost containing lime. Their compost should also be mixed with grit or even sand to provide good, sharp drainage, otherwise they may suffer from being waterlogged.

They can be watered well when they are in growth and fed occasionally. Use soft water as hard water contains lime and this will eventually have an adverse impact on the plant. If you live in a hard-water area, collect fresh rainwater and use that to water the plant. Watering in winter, when the plant is dormant, should be far more sparing: over watering can cause problems at this time.

Rhodohypoxis baurii

	SPRING	SUMMER	AUTUMN	WINTER	height (cm)	spread (cm)	flower colour	
Rhodohypoxis baurii		● ● ● ● / ● ● ● ● / ● ● ● ●			10	10		Parent of many good cultivars
R. baurii 'Albrighton'		● ● ● ● / ● ● ● ● / ● ● ● ●			10	10		Good strong coloured flowers
R. baurii 'Appleblossom'		● ● ● ● / ● ● ● ● / ● ● ● ●			10	10		Pretty pale pink flowers

● *flowering*

Rosa 'Rouletii'

Roses are so pretty, it seems a shame if they are only found in the garden. Rose plants are available which have the flower shapes, colours and scents of garden roses, but which have been bred to tolerate conservatory and greenhouse conditions.

Although they are just as happy to grow under glass, most of these plants have been bred to be sold as gifts and to be grown on as houseplants. Because of this they are generally far smaller than other roses and they make good, compact plants for growing under glass. The flowers are also much smaller than those of other roses, but they have lost little in the miniaturization process. Many are possibly prettier than their larger relatives.

Roses will bloom from early summer until the end of autumn, and are available in a wide range of colours. *Rosa* 'Rouletii' is a widely grown, particularly compact plant with deep pink, double flowers. There is a huge number of cultivars of roses suited to the conservatory or greenhouse, in a wide range of flower colours and with varying amounts of scent.

Rosa 'Rouletii'

All of the roses now grown as indoor plants have been bred from garden roses, so, like their garden relatives, they need lots of light in summer. Place them in a sunny spot and give them plenty of ventilation, particularly in warm weather.

soil	This plant will grow well if planted into a multi-purpose compost
temp	Requires cool greenhouse conditions with a minimum temperature of 4°C (39°F)
water & humidity	In summer water well. Water less in winter but do not allow to completely dry out. Mist regularly in summer
general care	Deadhead regularly to encourage flowers. Give the plant a good winter rest or place outside during winter
pests & diseases	Aphids, mildew, red spider mites, scale insect, die-back, downy mildew and viruses can all cause problems

Water freely throughout spring and summer, and into autumn. They are fairly greedy plants and should be fed every couple of weeks with a liquid fertilizer while they are in growth.

In winter, they will need a complete rest. Keep them cool and cut back on watering. They can be kept in a cool room over this time or can even be placed or planted out in the garden, as they are completely hardy. In this way they can be treated as a temporary conservatory plant. Bring them back inside once growth starts again in spring and re-pot or top-dress with fresh compost.

To keep the plants flowering repeatedly all through summer, deadhead any faded flowers regularly. This will encourage the regular formation of new buds. Leaves will drop naturally in autumn. After this has happened you can prune the plant back by about two thirds. You should also remove any stems that have died back naturally and any thin, weak or damaged stems. Flowers will be borne on the new growth that emerges the following spring.

Rosa 'Rouletii' mixed

Sarracenia

Like Nepenthes, Sarracenias are grown for their pitchers and are also known as pitcher plants. They are another carnivorous plant that originates in boggy conditions.

Carnivorous plants developed the features needed to catch and devour insects because of the almost sterile conditions in which they grow in the wild. They grow in mossy bogs that contain few nutrients. As they cannot gain nourishment from the soil, as most other plants do, they have had to find other ways to survive.

Sarracenia flava: close-up of pitcher

In Sarracenia, the method for catching prey is a pitcher, which is formed from a modified leaf, bent round on itself. At the top of the pitcher are glands that secrete nectar, and these lure insects inside. The inner walls of the pitcher are hard for insects to get a grip on, and they fall down into a well of liquid at the base of the pitcher and decompose, creating valuable nutrients for the plant.

Although macabre, these are fascinating plants to grow. Sarracenia is particularly ornamental as it produces spectacular flowers, as well as the pitchers. In *Sarracenia flava*, the pitchers are green and the flowers, which arrive in

Sarracenia flava

spring, are a greenish yellow. In *S. leucophylla* the pitchers have attractive white tops and the flowers are deep reddish-purple.

Sarracenias do not need high temperatures to thrive and they will do well in a greenhouse or conservatory that is kept just frost-free. In all but the harshest winters they will even do well in a cold greenhouse with no heating at all. However, they do require high levels of humidity and should be misted regularly and be placed in an area that is regularly damped down.

It is important that their growing medium and the water they are given are lime-free, as these are acid-loving plants. Use soft water when watering.

soil	Grow in an acidic mixture of sphagnum moss, coarse sand and leaf mould
temp	Requires cool greenhouse conditions with a minimum temperature of 4°C (39°F)
water & humidity	Keep moist in summer by standing in deep saucer of soft water. and slightly moist in winter. High humidity
general care	Feed with a liquid fertilizer once a month when the plant is in active growth during spring and summer
pests & diseases	Aphids, scale insect and mealy bugs can all attack and cause problems for Sarracenia plants

	SPRING	SUMMER	AUTUMN	WINTER	height (cm)	spread (cm)	flower colour	
Sarracenia flava	●●●				70	100		Spectacular yellow flowers produced
S. leucophylla	●●●				70	100		Deep red flowers and white tops to pitchers

● *flowering*

Saxifraga
Saxifrage

There are two types of saxifrage that are suitable for growing in greenhouses and conservatories, and both need quite different treatment.

Most are alpine plants with small, dense mounds of foliage that throw out colourful flowers in spring, and they need to be grown in a cold house or an alpine house. *Saxifraga stolonifera* 'Tricolor' is treated more like a houseplant and needs warm temperatures. It is grown for its foliage, which is rounded, hairy and brightly variegated.

In order for it to fully develop its pretty leaf colours, it should be placed in bright light and should be kept fairly dry. It does not like being waterlogged anyway and should always have good drainage, but the occasional absence of water seems to brighten the foliage colour. It needs warm conditions to grow well. It does not need high air humidity.

Flowers are produced in spring and summer, but they are fairly insignificant and

soil	Alpine compost for alpine types. Incorporate grit for *S. stolonifera* 'Tricolor'
temp	Minimum 10°C (50°F) for *S. stolonifera* 'Tricolor'. Cold or alpine greenhouse for others
water & humidity	Water *S. stolonifera* 'Tricolor.' Water alpines well in summer and keep almost dry in winter
general care	*S. stolonifera* 'Tricolor' develops best colour if kept slightly dry. Apply liquid feed once a month in summer
pests & diseases	Aphids and red spider mites can occur. Over watering or poor drainage can lead to crown rot

their presence reduces the production of new foliage so they should be removed.

Because of the production of runners the plant looks good in a hanging basket or in a pot on a shelf, where the runners can freely hang down. To propagate the plant, pin one of the runners down into a pot of compost and water it in. Once the new plant is established and is producing new growth, sever it from the parent.

Alpine plants are more mound-like in habit. They produce dense rosettes of foliage and small, pretty flowers that are held above the leaves. Keep in a cool greenhouse with plenty of ventilation, particularly in warm weather, and keep almost dry in winter. They can be watered fairly well during the growing season. They need an extremely well drained compost, and will grow best in a specially designed alpine compost.

Saxifraga stolonifera

	SPRING	SUMMER	AUTUMN	WINTER	height (cm)	spread (cm)	flower/leaf colour	
Saxifraga burseriana	● ●				5	15		Alpine saxifrage with pretty white flowers
S. 'Jenksiae'	● ● ●				5	20		Alpine type with pale pink flowers with dark pink centres
S. stolonifera 'Tricolor'					30	30		Neat habit and beautifully coloured leaves

● *flowering*

Schefflera
Umbrella plant

Schefflera plants are handsome, glossy-leaved, fast growing plants. They make great specimen plants and should be placed somewhere where their strong outline of umbrella-shaped leaves can be viewed.

Considering how impressive these plants can look, they are surprisingly easy to care for. They should be watered well in summer and less in winter, and should be misted regularly. They are fussy about temperature, and should be kept warm and away from draughts. They are best grown in hothouse conditions or in a warm conservatory. As they age, or if they are affected by low temperatures, they can often lose their leaves at the base of the stems.

They are commonly known as umbrella plants because of their whorls of leaves radiating from leaf stalks. *Schefflera actinophylla* has large green whorls of leaves. *S. arboricola* 'Variegata' is one of the more popular forms. It has the umbrella-shaped leaves but is also splashed with gold variegation in the centres of the leaflets. These plants can grow extremely large, and it can be hard to stop them from outgrowing their allotted space. They can also grow just a single stem, and this can make the plant look leggy and unattractive. Try pinching out the growing point while the plant is still young to encourage a more branching habit, although it is sometimes hard to encourage more than one stem to grow. Once a plant has outgrown its space, it can be pruned back and will re-shoot, although it can be better to take tip cuttings or try air layering to produce new plants.

S. elegantissima has a quite different look to the other plants. The leaves are so dark as to appear almost black. They are arranged in the same umbrella formation but have jagged edges. The plant is naturally bushier than the other scheffleras, but it can still grow extremely large.

soil	This plant will grow well in a well-drained multi-purpose compost
temp	Requires hot house conditions, minimum temperature of 16°C (61°F)
water & humidity	Water well during growing season, sparingly in winter. High humidity, particularly in warm weather
general care	Older stems can become bare as they mature and they are suitable for air layering in spring
pests & diseases	Scale insects, thrips and mealy bugs can occur. Leaf drop can be due to draughts or low humidity

Schefflera arboricola 'Variegata'

	SPRING	SUMMER	AUTUMN	WINTER	height (cm)	spread (cm)	leaf colour	
Schefflera actinophylla		● ● ●			250	100		Lovely glossy, mid-green leaves
S. arboricola 'Variegata'		● ● ●			250	100		Golden variegation to leaves
S. elegantissima					250	100		Black leaves with jagged edges

● *flowering*

Schlumbergera
Christmas cactus

Schlumbergera x buckleyi is commonly known as the Christmas cactus. With the right treatment it produces masses of its festively coloured red blooms on bright green leaves that brighten up the conservatory or greenhouse just in time for the Christmas holiday.

Schlumbergera x buckleyi

There are a number of different cultivars and species of Schlumbergera available that are also good for winter flowers. Some have different coloured flowers, including those in shades of purple, pink, white and orange. *Schlumbergera* 'Spectabile Coccineum' produces a huge amount of bright red flowers and has a particularly compact habit.

Unlike most cacti, Schlumbergera will grow best in a normal, multi-purpose compost with a little peat added. This is because their origins are in the forest, where it grows epiphytically on the branches of trees, rather than the desert, like the majority of cacti. They will usually be bought in flower and should be watered while the blooms last. After flowering, give plants a period of rest for a few weeks. This means cutting back on watering and keeping the compost almost completely dry.

In summer, the plant will benefit from a spell out of doors in a shady spot. This is when it will put on most of its new growth and it should be well watered over this time. Bring it into the greenhouse or conservatory in autumn before the weather turns cold. At this time plants can benefit from an application of fertiliser, which will help to encourage flower buds to form. Once these buds have started to form and to open, it is important not to move the plant or to place it in any draughts, as this can cause the buds to drop. It is also important to note that if the plant receives any artificial light in the evenings during the autumn months, flowering can be delayed.

soil	Will grow well in a multi-purpose compost with a little peat added
temp	Requires warm house conditions with a minimum temperature of 10°C (50°F)
water & humidity	Water well in summer. Needs a period of complete rest after flowering when it should not be watered
general care	Place outside for a spell during summer and allow to be watered by summer showers
pests & diseases	Mealy bugs can occur. Flowering can be delayed if plant receives artificial light during autumn evenings

Schlumbergera 'Spectabile Coccineum'

	SPRING	SUMMER	AUTUMN	WINTER	height (cm)	spread (cm)	flower colour	
Schlumbergera x buckleyi				● ●	35	80		Prized for its Christmas flowering
S. 'Spectabile Coccineum'	●			●	28	25		Compact and floriferous plant

● *flowering*

Conservatory & Greenhouse Plants

S

Strelitzia reginae

Bird of paradise

The flowers of *Strelitzia reginae* are spectacular. The plant is commonly called bird of paradise, and although it is tricky to work out exactly which part of a bird the flower is meant to represent (a bird in flight or the bill and head feathers?), there is no doubt that the flower has the colouring and shape to make such a comparison fair.

Strelitzia reginae

The flower spikes, which can grow up to 1.5m (5ft) in height, emerge from a clump of architectural, paddle-shaped mid-green leaves in spring. The tips of the flower spikes are made up from a green bract and are bent over. From the top of the crook emerge the bright orange and blue petals. The bracts themselves have a red stripe along them that adds to the colour and impact of the plant.

Mature plants will produce a succession of these flowers over several weeks in spring and early summer. Despite this impressive and exotic show, these plants are pretty easy to look after, as long as they can be kept warm during winter while they are dormant. They will need a temperature of at least 13°C (55°F) during this time, and so may be most suitable for growing in a conservatory that is kept warm all year round.

Young plants will not flower until they are a few years old, and these plants do not appreciate being given too much space to spread out into. They should be kept pot bound in order to get a really good show of flowers from them. However, they should be top dressed every spring. Only pot them on every three or four years.

They do not need a large amount of water, but should be watered moderately while actively growing. Keep them almost dry for the rest of the year, particularly during winter when they will go into a period of dormancy. When planting and potting on, make sure that the compost contains a large amount of grit for extra drainage, as these plants will suffer if they are over watered. Feed them once every month during the growing season with a liquid fertiliser. Light is important all year round, but provide a little shade from the hottest summer sun. Give full light in winter.

Propagation is fairly straightforward. Suckers are produced from around the base of the plant and these can be carefully prised away. Wait until you need to pot the plant on to do this, in order to keep disturbance of the plant to a minimum. Tease the suckers away from the main root ball and pot up in fresh compost.

soil	Will grow well in a multi-purpose compost with a little extra grit added
temp	Requires warm house conditions with a minimum temperature of 13°C (55°F)
water & humidity	Water well during the growing season and sparingly in winter. Requires average humidity
general care	Remove spent flowers regularly in order to encourage the growth of fresh flower spikes
pests & diseases	Mealy bugs and scale insects can cause problems. Poor drainage can lead to the development of crown rot

Conservatory & Greenhouse Plants

Streptocarpus

Cape primrose

Streptocarpus make extremely pretty, small, flowering plants for the greenhouse or conservatory. The Cape primroses, as they are commonly known, are compact and bright, and are available in a wide range of flower colours.

Streptocarpus 'Blushing Bride'

Most Cape primroses will flower throughout spring, summer and autumn. The flowers are borne on upright stems, often at least four or five to a stem. Thin tubes open up into five rounded petals, and the flowers have a strange backward sloping habit that makes them extremely distinctive. Leaves are long, dark green and slightly shiny.

Recent breeding has led to the development of huge numbers of new cultivars, which are becoming more widely available each year. Breeding has concentrated on developing plants with greater flowering abilities, and some, such as *Streptocarpus* 'Crystal Ice', can flower all year round. Breeding has also increased the different flower colours and forms and you can now buy plants with double flowers, such as *S.* 'Chorus Line', and plants with flowers in many different shades and colours.

Streptocarpus 'Crystal Ice'

Streptocarpus 'Chorus Line'

need a good, steady, fairly cool temperature but to be kept away from draughts. Keeping them in direct sunlight will lead to damaged leaves, but they do need good, bright, filtered light to flower at their best.

Be careful with watering. Waterlogged soil will lead to the base and stems rotting off, so allow the surface of the compost to dry off in between waterings. In winter watering should be even sparser. Slightly wet the compost occasionally, taking care not to splash the stems or base. In winter the compost should remain just moist.

soil	Will grow well in any well-drained multi-purpose compost
temp	Requires cool house conditions, minimum temperature of 4°C (39°F)
water & humidity	Water moderately in summer, leave compost surface to dry between waterings. Water sparingly in winter
general care	Needs re-potting every spring. After a few years, divide the plant to propagate and to keep it vigorous
pests & diseases	Mealy bugs, thrips and vine weevil. Over watering can lead to rotting of the stems and crown

Some of the prettiest flowers are those with fine, often dark blue or purple traced marks on pale petals. Compact cultivars are available that flower well but on extremely small rosettes of leaves.

Although they are popular, Streptocarpus plants can be difficult to look after. They

	SPRING	SUMMER	AUTUMN	WINTER	height (cm)	spread (cm)	flower colour	
Streptocarpus 'Blushing Bride'	● ●	● ● ●	● ●		20	45		Particularly compact plant with pretty flowers
S. 'Chorus Line'	● ●	● ● ●	● ●		20	45		Purple and white double flowers
S. 'Constant Nymph'	● ●	● ● ●	● ●		30	60		Good, long-established cultivar
S. 'Crystal Ice'	● ● ●	● ● ●	● ● ●	● ● ●	35	60		Can flower all year round

● *flowering*

Tibouchina urvilleana

Glory bush

Tibouchina urvilleana, commonly known as the glory bush, is a beautiful lax shrub that produces clear, vibrant purple flowers almost all year round. Their prominent stamens have given the plant its other common name of spider flower.

It originates in the rainforests of Mexico, but despite this does not need a particularly high temperature in order to thrive. It is best grown in a cool greenhouse or conservatory that is heated to keep it just above freezing point in winter. In warmer conditions than this it can continue to flower all year round. This is not necessarily a good thing however, as plants that are not given a winter rest can quickly burn themselves out. Force plants to rest by reducing temperature and watering from autumn onwards.

Tibouchina needs plenty of water throughout the growing season. Feed once a month with a liquid fertiliser over spring and summer. Good light is important, but they should have shade from the strongest of the summer sun. Plants will respond well to high temperatures in spring, summer and autumn by producing lots of flowers. However, at these times it is essential that they also have extremely good ventilation and high levels of humidity. Damp down the area around the

soil	Will perform well in any well-drained multi-purpose compost
temp	Requires cool house conditions with a minimum temperature of 4°C (39°F)
water & humidity	Water well in summer and sparingly in winter to force into a winter rest. High humidity in summer
general care	Pruning to keep plant down to size and in a good shape can be carried out in winter for this plant
pests & diseases	Aphids, red spider mite and oedema. Low light levels result in a lack of flowers. No other concerns

plant regularly throughout summer and mist the leaves in warm weather.

The evergreen foliage is attractive and covered in soft hairs. The flowers are borne on the ends of the stems. Plants in the wild will grow up to 6m (20ft) in height. While they will not reach these heights in containers, you will need to prune regularly to keep the plant down to size. This should be carried out in winter, after flowering has stopped. Do not prune back hard, but instead, shorten the longest growths and cut back some others a little more. If this is carried out every year the plant should be kept in check. Even though they are shrubs, they have such long, lax growths that they respond well to being trained as climbers. Train them in a fan shape against a wall or around a pillar.

It is important to pot Tibouchina plants on regularly to prevent them from getting root bound. Carry this out every couple of years, but pot on into a pot that is only slightly larger, to help keep the plant down to size. They will enjoy being grown directly in a border, but you will have to take care that they do not grow too large.

Tibouchina urvilleana

Trachelospermum

Trachelospermums are beautiful evergreen climbers that provide the glasshouse or conservatory with glossy dark green leaves all year round, and with pretty flowers in mid- and late summer.

Trachelospermum jasminoides

The flowers of *Trachelospermum asiaticum* are slightly creamy in colour and can have an almost yellow centre. Those of *T. jasminoides* are pure white. Both are beautifully scented and will fill the conservatory with their perfume. They are occasionally grown out of doors in areas that receive few frosts, as they can take fairly cool temperatures. However, they are at their best under the protection of a greenhouse or conservatory. They will grow well in a cold house with no heating at all, as this provides protection from the worst of winter weather. However, for best results grow in a cool house that is kept just frost-free.

These are great plants for training up a wall or around a pillar. They will need the support of a sturdy trellis or a set of horizontal wires. They climb by twining their stems around whatever support is available, but it can be a good idea to tie them in from time to time to encourage a neat habit. Whenever you notice a few stray stems that have not attached themselves to the support, tie them in loosely with some soft twine.

Trachelospermums grow too large for most conservatories, and should be pruned regularly to keep them down to size. The best time to do this is in early spring, before the new growth begins. Avoid cutting the plant back too hard, and instead reduce the individual branches. Flowers are formed on the previous year's growth, and so cutting back too hard can lead to a year with no flowers.

Grow in a spot that receives a good amount of sunlight but that has a little shade from direct sun in mid-summer. Although a multi-purpose compost can be used, these plants appreciate the addition of a little leaf mould.

soil	Grows best in well-drained, multi-purpose compost with added leaf mould
temp	Requires cool house conditions with a minimum temperature of 4°C (39°F)
water & humidity	Water well during the growing season, moderately during winter months. Needs average humidity
general care	Prune the plant annually in order to keep it down to size. The best time to do this is in spring
pests & diseases	Trachelospermum may take a little time to get established, but there are no other concerns

	SPRING	SUMMER	AUTUMN	WINTER	height (cm)	spread (cm)	flower colour	
Trachelospermum asiaticum		● ●			600	200		Scented cream coloured flowers
T. jasminoides		● ●			900	300		Slow-growing evergreen climber

● *flowering*

Trachycarpus fortunei

Chusan palm *or* windmill palm

Trachycarpus is commonly known as the Chusan palm or as the windmill palm, because of the fan-like shape of its leaves. It is an impressive foliage plant for the greenhouse or conservatory, particularly when it is still small.

Trachycarpus fortunei

In many areas that do not receive hard frosts, Trachycarpus plants are grown out of doors. In fact, Trachycarpus is almost hardy, but it needs protection from the hardest frosts and the worst winter weather. Its leaves are also prone to becoming tattered and shredded if the plants are grown in windy spots, and so the plant tends to look better if it is grown under protection. There its large leaves can be shown off to their full glory.

Drainage is important to all palms, and the compost that Trachycarpus is planted into should be mixed into a good amount of grit. It is also a good idea to create a drainage layer at the bottom of the pot. This can consist of broken crocks to cover the drainage holes and prevent them from clogging up with compost, as well as a layer of grit to help water drain quickly away. These plants will really suffer if they are left waterlogged.

Ideally they should be placed in a spot in light shade and should definitely be given protection from strong summer sunshine. They will need feeding about once a month with a liquid feed throughout the growing season. They never need huge amounts of water, but should be watered fairly well throughout the growing season and will need a good amount of humidity in warm weather. In winter, take care to reduce watering.

As Trachycarpus plants grow, their leaves form a central stem. Eventually, the older leaves towards the bottom of the stem will die off. This is all part of the plant's natural growth process and is not cause for alarm. These dead leaves should be cut off near their base. They will then help to form part of the stem. As these plants age, the stem becomes longer and more visible. This is a good thing in a landscape situation, but up close, in a greenhouse or conservatory, the stems can look a little ugly. Therefore it can be a good idea to replace old plants with young ones. Suckers are regularly produced at the base of the plant and these can be teased away from the root ball and potted up in fresh compost.

soil	Will grow well in a deep container of well-drained multi-purpose compost
temp	Requires cool house conditions with a minimum temperature of 4°C (39°F)
water & humidity	Water moderately during the growing season, sparingly in winter. Needs high humidity in warm weather
general care	These palms will appreciate a spell out of doors during summer. They should not be potted on too frequently
pests & diseases	Scale insects, red spider mite and aphids can all attack and cause problems for Trachycarpus plants

Trachycarpus fortunei

Conservatory & Greenhouse Plants

139

Veltheimia

Veltheimia is a pretty greenhouse or conservatory bulb. It produces its flowers, which are very similar to those of Kniphofia, the red-hot poker, in spring.

Veltheimia bracteata is fairly easy to grow, but *V. capensis* is a little trickier. Veltheimia is a plant that originates in South Africa and naturally grows in rocky habitats. Because of this it appreciates extremely good drainage and will suffer if its roots are allowed to sit in water. An excellent idea is to mix a good amount of sharp sand in with its compost, to help the water to drain away more quickly. You should also put broken crocks in the bottom of the containers to prevent compost from blocking up the drainage holes and preventing good drainage. Sun is important and it should be placed in a spot where it receives full light for as long as possible.

soil	Will grow well in a well-drained multi-purpose compost with added sand
temp	Requires cool house conditions with a minimum temperature of 6°C (43°F)
water & humidity	Water fairly well when in growth. When dormant keep *V. bracteata* just moist and *V. capensis* dry
general care	Grow this plant in full sun for best flowering. Pot on only when plant is root bound
pests & diseases	Veltheimia is fairly trouble free and is not attacked by any particular pest or disease

Veltheimia bracteata

Bulbs are planted in autumn for spring flowering. When the leaves begin to grow watering should be carried out carefully. These leaves are attractive in their own right, and are glossy, wavy and dark green in *V. bracteata* and glaucous in *V. capensis*. When the plant is in full growth it can be watered fairly well, and should be fed once a fortnight with a liquid fertiliser. After flowering is over the leaves will gradually die back, and over this time watering should be gradually reduced. When completely dormant, the bulbs of *V. capensis* should be kept completely dry, while those of *V. bracteata* can be kept just slightly moist. At no time do they need particularly high humidity.

Propagation is by seed in a heated propagator or by offsets. These can be removed when the plant is occasionally potted up, in autumn, and should be potted up into fresh compost.

	SPRING	SUMMER	AUTUMN	WINTER	height (cm)	spread (cm)	flower colour	
Veltheimia bracteata	● ● ●		🛠 🛠 🛠					Clusters of dark pink flowers on a tall stem
V. capensis	● ● ●		🛠 🛠 🛠					Variable colouring and patterned flowers

🛠 *planting*   ● *flowering*

Yucca

Yucca is an easy plant to grow for impressive, architectural foliage in the greenhouse or conservatory. It has sword-like, evergreen leaves and can even produce large spikes of white flowers.

Yucca elephantipes 'Variegata'

Yucca elephantipes

Yuccas are desert plants from Central America and so like to be grown in full light. They also need good drainage and should not be over watered at any time of year, but should be allowed to get fairly dry in winter.

Many yuccas are almost hardy and they are often seen growing out of doors in areas that do not have harsh winters. Others, however, fare better under the protection of glass.

Yucca elephantipes is a green leaved species that has a good, branching shape. As it ages it develops long stems, all clothed in the long, spiky leaves. Its cultivar, *Y. elephantipes* 'Variegata' has a similar habit but with a pale cream stripe along the outside of each leaf. This makes the plant more impressive and attractive.

As they are nearly hardy, they do not need to be grown in high temperatures and may even grow well in an unheated cold house, which will protect plants from the worst of winter weather. However, they will do best in a cool greenhouse that is heated in winter to keep it just above freezing.

Mature plants – those around four or five years old – will produce flowers. These are extremely impressive. They are white and bell-shaped, and are borne densely on tall spikes. Unless you wish the plant to produce seed, cut these flower spikes off once they have faded to prevent the plant from putting all its energy into seed production. It is easier to propagate the plant from suckers, which appear near the base of the plant.

soil	Will grow best in any well-drained multi-purpose compost
temp	Requires cool house conditions with a minimum temperature of 5°C (41°F)
water & humidity	Water carefully during the growing season and sparingly in winter. Low humidity
general care	Yuccas will appreciate a spell out of doors in summer, where they can be placed in full sun
pests & diseases	Aphids can attack flowers and may occasionally cause problems on the young growth of yucca plants

	SPRING	SUMMER	AUTUMN	WINTER	height (cm)	spread (cm)	leaf colour	
Yucca elephantipes		● ● ●			800	300		Impressive architectural shape
Y. elephantipes 'Variegata'		● ● ●			800	300		Leaves have cream variegation along edges

● *flowering*

Zantedeschia
Calla lily

Zantedeschia aethiopica, commonly known as the calla lily, is a widely grown plant in boggy areas in gardens as it is fairly hardy.

Zantedeschias may seem to be strange plants to include in the greenhouse or conservatory as they grow in boggy conditions, but they do appreciate a little protection and may suffer in harsher winters out of doors. There are, however, a number of particularly colourful and choice Zantedeschias that are not hardy, and these can only be grown under glass.

The flowers of Zantedeschia are unusual. What many people consider to be the flower is, in fact, called a spathe. These are single, petal-like structures that are wrapped around the tops of the flower spikes. The true flowers are tiny and cover the central spike that is found inside the spathe.

The spathes of *Zantedeschia aethiopica* are pure white and it has bright green foliage. *Z. elliottiana* is a species with particularly attractive foliage, covered in small white dots. The spathes are yellow.

soil	This plant will grow well if it is grown in a multi-purpose compost
temp	Cold house conditions for *Z. aethiopica*. Minimum 10°C (50°F) for others
water & humidity	Water Zantedeschias well during the growing season and keep moist in winter. Average humidity
general care	Pot on every year, preferably in autumn. Plants can be divided for propagation at the same time
pests & diseases	Aphids can attack and cause problems for Zantedeschia, particularly on younger more tender growth

The most colourful of the species is *Z. rehmannii*, which has dark pink or purple spathes.

In their natural habitat in South Africa these are bog plants, and so it follows that they need to be kept well watered all year round. In fact, in winter, they should be kept just moist, but in summer they should be watered freely. They do not need particularly high levels of humidity, however. Regular feeding, about every week with a liquid feed during summer, will help to keep plants flowering well. They like to be grown in good light, but can suffer from leaf browning if they are not given shade from the harsh midday summer sun.

Propagation is by division, which should be carried out every three years or so, otherwise flowering can be affected. Lift and split the plants and re-pot into fresh compost.

Zantedeschia aethiopica

	SPRING	SUMMER	AUTUMN	WINTER	height (cm)	spread (cm)	flower colour	
Zantedeschia aethiopica	● ● ●				90	60	☐	Large, pure white spathes
Z. elliottiana		● ● ●			80	20	☐	Patterned leaves and yellow spathes
Z. rehmannii		● ● ●			40	30	■	Compact plant with pink spathes

● *flowering*

Conservatory & Greenhouse

Edibles

Greenhouses have always been used for growing edible plants. The traditional image of a gardener in their greenhouse is one of tending tomatoes and cucumbers. There is still a place for these crops in the greenhouse and even the conservatory. There are a number of older 'heritage' cultivars that produce particularly unusual or colourful fruits, and these would look good mixed in among flowering plants.

There are many plants that have been grown under glass for decades, and that are still well worth trying. Grape vines and citrus trees are almost as ornamental as they are useful. They bring to the domestic greenhouse some of the grandeur of the Victorian kitchen garden or orangery.

However, in addition to these stalwarts there are many more unusual edible plants that can be introduced to the greenhouse and conservatory. The extra protection that both afford allow the gardener to experiment with crops that are reminiscent of the tropics and might previously have been restricted to gardeners in warm climates. Okra, Cape gooseberry and pineapple can all be grown and successfully fruited under glass, and all make an exotic and impressive addition to the usual garden produce.

Whether you dedicate your greenhouse to edibles or mix in some of the more attractive plants with your ornamentals, it would seem a missed opportunity not to grow something edible. If you have time and patience, go for the more demanding annual vegetable plants, such as aubergines. If you want something involving little effort but giving you something attractive, as well as the occasional fruit, choose a citrus tree or an olive. There is an edible plant to suit every level of knowledge and every taste.

Tomatoes *Lycopersicon esculentum*

Tomatoes are hugely popular plants that are widely grown under glass. They do not make particularly attractive plants in their own right, and so are perhaps best suited to the greenhouse rather than the conservatory. One of the reasons that so many people grow tomatoes is that there is a wide range of varieties that can be grown from seed. Most of these are not sold as fruits in shops, and so growing at home opens up a large number of flavours, shapes and colours that would not otherwise be available. Another reason so many people grow them is that the flavour of all homegrown tomatoes tends to be so much better than those bought in shops.

You can start seeds off in early spring in small pots of seed and cutting compost, or you can buy young plants later in the year. Grow in a cool greenhouse that is kept frost-free in spring when seeds are germinating. Growing from seed will make a wider range of plants available. Plant young plants into grow bags or large pots filled with well-drained multi-purpose compost. It is important to keep tomato plants well watered throughout summer, and so the larger the amount of soil they have available to them, the less likely they are to dry out. Do not grow tomatoes directly in your greenhouse border, however, as you will be

unable to plant them there the following year in case of soil-borne diseases. Make sure the soil is constantly moist, but not soggy.

Plants grown out of doors will be pollinated by insects, but this will not happen in a greenhouse. To aid pollination, tap the flowering stems to encourage the movement of pollen. You can also mist the flowers to aid fruit set. Use a specially formulated tomato fertilizer feed once a fortnight.

Tomatoes have two main habits: bush types have a sturdy, bushy habit while cordon types grow tall and thin. Both types should be supported as they grow by tying in to a bamboo cane, pushed into the compost. Cordon tomatoes will need to have their side shoots removed as they grow, otherwise the plant will keep producing new, leafy growths and may not ripen fruits well. Pinch out the tops when a number of fruits have started to set, in order to concentrate the plant's energy on the existing fruits. Bush types will not need pinching out. Watch out for aphids, mosaic virus, botrytis, blossom end rot and foot rot.

Plant: start seeds in late winter up until mid-spring **Harvest:** fruits are ready for most varieties in late summer to early autumn; 'Blizzard' variety starts fruiting mid-summer until early autumn **Varieties:** Tomato 'Big Boy' – a beefsteak-type tomato with large, juicy fruits; Tomato 'Blizzard' – a small variety with early, bright-red fruits; Tomato 'Nectar' – a variety that is resistant to viruses; Tomato 'San Marzano' – a heavy cropping plum tomato.

Peppers *Capsicum annuum*

Peppers are a great edible plant to grow in either the conservatory or greenhouse as they are ornamental, as well as producing tasty fruits. They make compact bushy plants that can be completely covered in small colourful fruits.

The sweet peppers are perhaps slightly less ornamental than the chilli or hot peppers, which produce many small fruits. Sweet peppers produce fewer and larger fruits, but are still attractive plants. All peppers can be harvested and eaten at any stage, but their properties change radically as they mature. The fruits of sweet peppers become sweeter and turn from green to shades of red, purple and orange as they ripen. Hot peppers turn from green to red, yellow or purple and become spicier as they ripen. There are many different types available, from those that will add a mild spiciness to a dish, to others that will add an eye-watering heat.

Peppers are grown in a similar way to tomatoes, and should be sown in early spring, in a cool, frost-free greenhouse for germination, then planted out into pots containing well-drained multi-purpose compost or grow bags in late spring, and harvested from late summer onwards. They will need to be kept well watered but not soggy, and should be fed every two weeks. It can be a good idea to use a tomato fertilizer once a fortnight, as this has been specially formulated to encourage good flower and fruit formation. All peppers will grow best and ripen fruits most successfully if they are grown in a warm spot in full sun. They will appreciate a fairly high level of humidity, particularly when the fruits are setting, and so should be in a greenhouse or conservatory that is damped down regularly during summer. The fruits of all types will ripen after they have been picked. Picking unripe fruits regularly can help to encourage the plant to keep producing new fruits, and so can increase yield. Watch out for pests and diseases; aphids, red spider mite and blossom end rot can all attack and cause problems for pepper plants.

Plant: start seeds in early spring – Pepper 'Gypsy', 'Jalapeno' and 'Red Cherry' up until mid-spring
Harvest: fruits are best picked late summer to early autumn **Varieties:** Pepper 'Hungarian Hot Wax' (*top*) – mild hot pepper in yellow and red; Pepper 'Jalapeno' – mid-heat hot pepper with shiny green skin; Pepper 'Rainbow' – sweet peppers produced in many different colours; Pepper 'Red Cherry' (*bottom*) – bears many small, fiercely hot fruits.

Vines *Vitis vinifera*

Grapes are hardy and can be grown out of doors in areas that receive frosts. However, in all but the warmest areas, it can be hard to ripen fruits and so they are the perfect addition to a productive conservatory or greenhouse.

As well as producing delicious fruits, vines are useful plants as they can be trained to grow up and along the inside of roof ridges. The attractive, deciduous leaves then provide shade in hot summer weather, but fall in autumn to allow lots of winter light.

Both dessert and wine vines are available, but as you would need to produce such a large amount of grapes to make wine, it seems sensible to use the greenhouse or conservatory for the production of tasty dessert grapes. There are three different types available: vinous, sweetwater and muscat. Vinous types are the least tasty, but are fairly easy to grow. Sweetwaters ripen early and have fairly good flavour, and muscats have the best flavour of all but ripen early. If you are growing vines in an unheated cold house or cool greenhouse it makes sense to opt for an early maturing cultivar, as the heat of the sun in summer will then be adequate to ripen the fruits. Later ripening cultivars may need to be

grown in heated glasshouses, as they will not ripen until autumn, when weather can turn cold.

Vines like to have cool roots, so it can be a good idea to plant the roots of the plant outside the glasshouse and feed the stem indoors. The planting hole should be well prepared and have plenty of well-rotted manure added.

Pruning is essential and can be complicated. If you are aiming to grow the vine along the ridge of the greenhouse roof, go for single cordon pruning. This will create a single stem that produces short, fruiting growths each year. Growth should be pruned back to the central stem each winter when the plant is dormant. You can create a multiple cordon by first training two growths horizontally and then selecting vertical growths to grow as cordons.

As soon as fruits have set, thin them so that there is only one bunch per 12cm (1ft) of stem. Each bunch will also need many of the individual fruits removing, otherwise each fruit will stay relatively small. Use scissors to remove all of the smaller fruits on each bunch, leaving enough space between the larger grapes for them to swell to their full size. Watch out for powdery mildew and red spider mite.

Plant: any time from mid-autumn until late winter **Harvest:** fruits are ready to be harvested from mid-autumn until mid-winter **Varieties:** Grape 'Alicante' – late maturing black-purple, vinous type; Grape 'Foster's Seedling' – early maturing, white, sweetwater type of vine; Grape 'Muscat of Alexandria' (*above*) – late maturing, white muscat type.

Citrus plants, such as mandarins, tangerines, oranges, lemons and limes, have become popular for growing under glass and more cultivars are constantly being made available. This is possibly because they are such good-looking plants. They have dark, glossy, evergreen leaves and can produce their fragrant flowers and colourful fruit all year round, often at the same time as each other. They sometimes produce fruits in winter, when other plants are not looking their best.

There are a number of different types available. Of these, limes and lemons are among the most compact and prettiest, and so are the most suitable for the smaller conservatory or greenhouse. However, if you have the space, you can grow almost any type of citrus you like. Grow in well-drained, slightly acidic compost.

They do not necessarily require high temperatures, and will survive in greenhouses that are kept at just above freezing (5°C/41°F). However, flowering is related to temperature, so if you want flowers to be produced all winter, you may have to provide higher winter temperatures. Fruits can take a long time to ripen, and those that are on the tree over winter will be the result of summer flowers.

As these plants can grow all year round, it is important to water and feed them year round as well. Special citrus fertilizers are available. Water with soft water to help keep the compost acidic. If you live in a hard-water area, use freshly collected rainwater for this. They like high levels of light all year round, and a good deal of direct sunlight. They can benefit from a spell out of doors in summer.

Prune plants for shape, after fruiting. You should aim to shorten any long, sappy growths so that all growths are sturdy and able to support the weight of the fruit. Do not pot on too frequently, and take care to use a lime-free compost when you do. Watch out for scales insects, red spider mite and aphids.

Plant: any time during the year **Flower:** all year round, depending on temperature **Harvest:** fruits can be harvested all year round, depending on temperature, often ripening from early to late winter **Varieties:** *Citrus* 'Meyer' – a compact lemon cultivar; *Citrus reticulata* 'Clementine' – a mandarin or tangerine with fragrant flowers; *Citrus sinensis* 'Valencia' – a sweet orange that can grow up to 3m (10ft) high; *Citrus aurantium* 'Seville' – a bitter orange, reaching heights of 6m (21ft) if allowed; *Citrus aurantifolia* 'West Indian' – a popular lime with good, sharp taste.

Pomegranates are extremely ornamental trees that produce bright red flowers followed by round, pink fruits full of juicy seeds. They can tolerate frosts for a short while but are best grown in a cool house kept frost-free throughout winter. Heating into autumn may be necessary to bring fruits to full ripeness. *Punica granatum* var. *nana* is a particularly useful plant as it is very compact but still produces masses of fruits.

Provide a large pot filled with well-drained, loam-based soil or plant out into a greenhouse or conservatory border. Place in a spot that receives full sun. Water well throughout the growing season and keep fairly dry in winter. Feed with a liquid fertilizer every couple of weeks in spring and summer. Prune to create a good framework and then to keep down to size, to keep the framework fairly open and to get rid of dead and diseased growth. Pomegranates can be affected by scale insects, aphids, red spider mites and thrips.

Plant: early to late spring **Flower:** early to late summer **Harvest:** fruits are ready early to late autumn **Varieties:** *Punica granatum* – large plant with bright-red flowers; *Punica granatum* var. *nana* – compact, peachy pink variety that produces lots of fruit.

Peach *Prunus persica* **Nectarine** *P. persica* var. *nectarina* **Apricot** *P. armeniaca*

Although peaches and nectarines are both hardy plants, they are unlikely to produce much fruit if grown outside in a frost-prone climate. The slight protection afforded by a cool greenhouse, kept at just above freezing (4°C/39°F), is the perfect environment for them. Apricots need protection from frost and also do well under glass.

Both peaches and nectarines produce blossom early in the year, and this can be ruined by frosts, which in turn can lead to a disappointing crop. A major problem suffered by peaches out of doors is peach leaf curl. This is a fungus that is carried in rainwater, and so simply by growing under glass and preventing rain from falling on the plants, you eliminate the source of the problem.

Grow peaches and nectarines in fertile, well-cultivated border soil. Water well when flowering or fruiting and during warm spells. Train them in a fan shape against a sunny wall and prune in winter, removing old growths and allowing the previous year's shoots to establish. Hand pollinate the flowers in spring by brushing them carefully with a soft paintbrush. Dwarf plants are excellent for conservatories and can be grown in large containers.

Apricots produce delicious, juicy, golden yellow fruit in early autumn. Although they are related to peaches and nectarines, they do not like the same richness of soil, so make sure they are planted into a well-drained, fairly poor soil. Fan training against a warm, sunny wall suits them well. When pruning in winter, concentrate on cutting out older wood and on keeping the previous season's growths, as these will be the most productive. Train the new growths into place over summer so that they will replace the older ones. Aid pollination by carefully brushing the centres of the flowers with a soft paintbrush. You will need to thin out the fruit as it begins to develop, otherwise you will be left with lots of small, unripe fruit at the end of the year. Apricots do not need large amounts of fertilizer throughout the year. Watch out for attack by rust, as well as die back.

Plant: during spring for peaches and nectarines; late autumn/early winter for apricots **Flower:** mid- to late spring **Harvest:** fruits are ready to be harvested from mid-summer until early autumn **Varieties:** Peach 'Bonanza' – dwarf cultivar, suited to containers; Nectarine 'Early Rivers' – orange-red, good flavoured nectarine; Apricot 'Hemskerk' – popular cultivar with good flavour.

Olive *Olea europaea*

Olives are natives of the Mediterranean, and there are few trees that can evoke the region so well. They have attractive silvery leaves and produce small green fruits that turn black on ripening. They can be grown outdoors in frost-prone climates, in fact they even require a period of cold, but they will only produce edible fruits in long, hot summers. Due to their cold requirement they are best grown in an unheated cold house, but will appreciate high temperatures in summer.

Olives will grow happily in a large container in well-drained soil, fairly low in nutrients. Water well throughout summer, but keep humidity low when flowering. Feed occasionally with a liquid fertilizer. Prune to create a strong framework, removing old growth each year. Fruits are produced on the previous year's growth. Pests include thrips and red spider mites.

Plant: any time **Flower:** all summer **Harvest:** during the autumn **Varieties:** Olive 'El Greco' – popular cultivar with good flavoured olives; Olive 'Manzanillo' – produces particularly tasty fruit.

Fig *Ficus carica*

As well as producing delicious fruits, figs are attractive trees to grow under glass, with glossy, deciduous leaves. Grow in a cool house that is kept frost-free over winter. It is essential that the roots of figs are contained, otherwise they will grow too large. Grow in a pot or, if planting into a border, line the hole with concrete slabs. The base should be filed with rubble. The poorer the soil you are able to provide, the more tough, fruiting wood will be produced.

As figs are large growers, it can be a good idea to train them as a fan against a wall. Make sure that it is a wall that receives lots of sun. Space the branches well to allow room for the foliage. Each year, prune out old wood and tie younger branches into their place. You can also remove the tips of growths to stop them growing too long and to encourage the production of fruiting wood. Water well in summer. Pests include red spider mites and mealy bugs.

Plant: mid- to late spring in cool areas, late autumn elsewhere **Harvest:** fruits are ready to harvest from late summer to early autumn **Varieties:** *Ficus carica* 'White Marseilles' (*above*) – best grown under glass.

Strawberry *Fragaria x ananassa*

Strawberries can be grown out of doors, but it is possible to force plants into producing fruits up to one month early by growing them in a heated greenhouse or conservatory. Even plants grown in an unheated house will provide delicious fruits well before those in the garden are ready for eating.

Pot up strawberry plants using garden soil in autumn and leave them in a sheltered spot in the garden. Bring them indoors in early or mid-winter and, if it is a heated house, gradually increase the heat. When flowers appear there will be no natural pollinators around, so use a soft paintbrush to gently brush each flower in turn, so transferring pollen from one plant to the next.

Red spider mite can be a big problem and can be kept down by high levels of humidity. Water plants carefully as they are starting into growth, and then freely as fruits begin to form and ripen. Plant forced strawberry plants out into the garden after fruiting and do not use them again for forcing.

Plant: during the autumn months outside and bring inside early to mid-winter **Harvest:** fruits are ripe for picking from late spring to early summer **Varieties:** Strawberry 'Cambridge Favourite' – heavy yields and well-suited for growing under glass; Strawberry 'Royal Sovereign' – an old cultivar with a good flavour.

Cape gooseberry *Physalis edulis*

Cape gooseberries are unusual fruits that should be grown as annuals. In autumn they produce small tangy, orange fruits concealed in attractive papery cases. Grow in a cool greenhouse that receives a little heat during cooler weather.

Sow seeds in early spring and plant out in late spring. You will need to provide a large pot as these plants can grow up to 1.8m (6ft) in height. You can keep them more manageable, and encourage a better-shaped plant, by regularly nipping out the growing tips. It is a good idea to provide some support for the plant, and to tie it in regularly as it grows. Water well throughout summer, and start feeding once fruits are visible. You should then feed with a liquid tomato fertilizer every two weeks until the fruits have ripened in autumn. Aphids can attack plants through summer. Once you have harvested all of the fruits, you should discard the plant.

Plant: sow in early spring and plant out in late spring **Harvest:** fruits are ready for harvesting from early to mid-autumn.

Pineapple *Ananus comosus*

Pineapples are delicious tropical fruits that are fun to grow in a conservatory or warm greenhouse. Children in particular enjoy rooting and growing them.

They will need fairly high temperatures if they are to thrive and fruit. Grow in a warm or hot greenhouse or in a conservatory that is kept at a minimum temperature of 16°C (61°F) in winter. You may be able to track down plants from specialist conservatory and house plant nurseries, or you can root your own from a pineapple you have eaten. Cut off a small section of the top of the plant, including the leaves. Place into a small pot of compost and keep warm and well watered. Once plants have rooted they can be potted on into a larger pot. New plants will take up to two years to produce flowers; the fruits may take up to six months to fully ripen.

They like high levels of humidity and need to be watered well in summer. Keep the central funnel of the plant at least half filled with water during the growing season. Mealy bugs and scale insects can attack and cause problems.

Plant: any time, as long as the temperature is above 16°C (61°F) **Flower:** early to late summer
Harvest: fruits are ready for harvesting in early autumn.

Ginger *Zingiber officinale*

Edible ginger makes an attractive plant and, if grown well, the root can swell to provide ginger for cooking and teas.

Buy a large piece of ginger and leave it in a sunny spot until it sprouts. Plant it close to the surface of a shallow pot filled with multi-purpose compost with lots of horticultural grit or perlite added. Given warmth and plenty of indirect light it will soon start to produce leaves. The leaves that emerge from the stems are slim and glossy dark-green with a tropical appearance. If given warmth they may eventually produce yellow and purple flowers, but this is rare. Keep the soil moist, but try to avoid wetting the root directly as this can lead to rots.

In autumn, the foliage will die down, and this is a good time to harvest. The root should have swelled to several times its original size. Place it in a sunny spot and turn several times to allow the surface to dry out. This will help it to store well.

Plant: any time **Flower:** mid-summer **Harvest:** mid-autumn.

Okra *Abelomoschus esculentus*

Okra is an unusual vegetable, widely used in Indian cuisine. The pods are best picked and eaten before they are fully mature.

Sow seeds after soaking them for 24 hours. Once they have germinated, grow them on before planting them out into grow bags or large containers. The plants will need warmth and humidity to grow and produce well, so damp the greenhouse down often. Water well and feed every two weeks; pinch out the growing tips to encourage a bushy habit. Harvest the pods as soon as they have grown 5–8cm (2–3in) in length roughly 10 weeks after the seeds were sown. The younger the pods are, the more succulent and tasty they will be. Okra can be attacked by red spider mite and aphids.

Plant: sow mid- to late spring **Harvest:** late summer to early autumn.

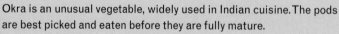

Melon *Cucumis melo* **Cucumber** *Cucumis sativus*

Melons can be grown successfully in a glasshouse or polytunnel that receives no extra heat. The additional shelter afforded by being under cover ought to be enough to ripen these delicious and juicy fruits.

They will need some heat when seeds are germinating and should be sown two to a pot in a heated propagator. Once seeds have germinated, remove the weaker and grow on in the greenhouse. About one month after germination, the seedlings should be ready to plant out into grow bags or large pots. Do not plant directly into the greenhouse border. When flowers appear, hand pollinate them using a soft paintbrush. Pollen from a male flower must be transferred to the female flowers. Identify the females by the swelling behind the flower. Stop growth of the main stem and side shoots when they have about three leaves each, otherwise all energy will go into producing lush growth. Harvest fruits when they start to smell sweet.

Cucumber is a classic greenhouse vegetable and does not need heat to grow well and for fruits to mature. It is an essential ingredient in summer salads.

Sow seeds in pots in a heated propagator in spring, two to a pot. Once they have germinated, remove the weaker seedling. Transfer into a grow bag or large pot of soil. These plants will need support. Use tall canes or netting and tie them in as they grow. Stop growth once it has reached the top of the support. Feed and water regularly, taking particular care once flowers and fruits have started to appear. Damp down around the plants to keep humidity high. Nip out side growths regularly to prevent the plant from putting on too much green growth at the expense of fruits. Harvesting should begin about three months after seed sowing.

Plant: early to late spring **Flower:** mid-summer to early autumn (melons); mid-summer to mid-autumn (cucumbers) **Harvest:** mid-summer to early autumn (melons); mid-summer to mid-autumn (cucumbers) **Varieties:** Melon 'Blenheim Orange' – dark orange, musk melon with good taste; Melon 'Sweetheart' – early maturing cantaloupe melon; Cucumber 'Birgit' – heavy crops early in season; Cucumber 'Pepita' – many small fruits produced; Cucumber 'Telegraph Improved' – old popular cultivar.

Aubergine *Solanum melongena*

Aubergine is a delicious vegetable with many uses that is easily grown in an unheated glasshouse. There are many different cultivars available and many have particularly attractive fruits.

They are grown in a similar way to tomatoes and are in fact related as both are members of the Solanaceae family. The seeds should be sown in a warm spot in a small pot in early spring and then planted out as soon as they are large enough into a grow bag or large pot of multi-purpose compost. As soon as fruits appear the plant should be fed regularly, every week, with a tomato fertilizer. The fruits can take a long time to fully ripen and it can be a good idea to restrict the number of fruits on each plant. With some larger fruited cultivars this may mean keeping just five or six fruits. Harvest towards the end of summer. Plants can be attacked by red spider mite, aphids and powdery mildew.

Plant: early to late spring **Harvest:** fruits ready for harvesting from mid-summer to early autumn **Varieties:** Aubergine 'Black Beauty' – purple-black, glossy fruits mature early; Aubergine 'Easter Egg' – egg-shaped, pale fruits.

Troubleshooting

Growing a varied range of plants under glass attracts an equally varied selection of pests, diseases and other problems. The following diagram is designed to help you diagnose conditions suffered by your plants from the symptoms you can observe. Starting with the part of the plant that appears to be the most affected, by answering successive questions 'yes' [✓] or 'no' [✗] you will quickly arrive at a probable cause. Once you have identified the cause, turn to the relevant entry in the directory of pests and diseases for details of how to treat the problem.

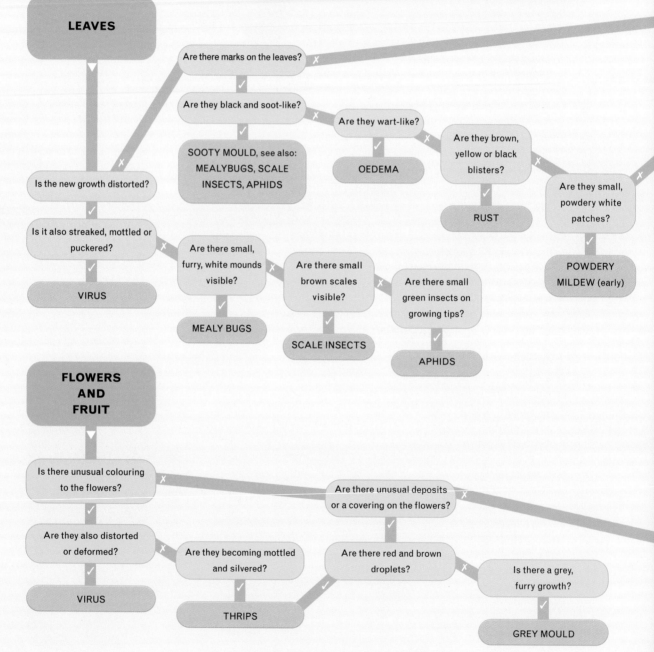

LEAVES

Are there marks on the leaves?

Are they black and soot-like?

Are they wart-like?

Are they brown, yellow or black blisters?

SOOTY MOULD, see also: MEALYBUGS, SCALE INSECTS, APHIDS

OEDEMA

Are they small, powdery white patches?

RUST

Is the new growth distorted?

POWDERY MILDEW (early)

Is it also streaked, mottled or puckered?

Are there small, furry, white mounds visible?

Are there small brown scales visible?

Are there small green insects on growing tips?

VIRUS

MEALY BUGS

SCALE INSECTS

APHIDS

FLOWERS AND FRUIT

Is there unusual colouring to the flowers?

Are there unusual deposits or a covering on the flowers?

Are they also distorted or deformed?

Are they becoming mottled and silvered?

Are there red and brown droplets?

Is there a grey, furry growth?

VIRUS

THRIPS

GREY MOULD

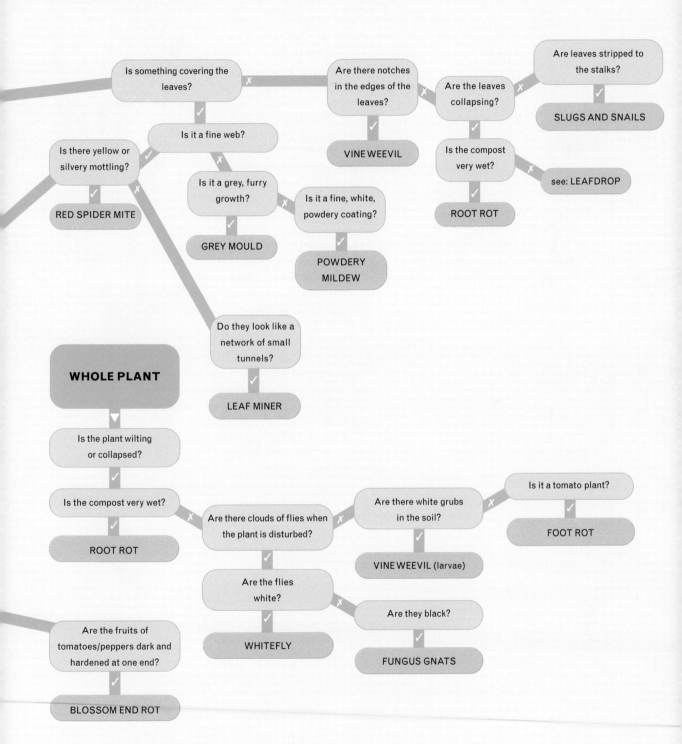

Is something covering the leaves?

Are there notches in the edges of the leaves?

Are the leaves collapsing?

Are leaves stripped to the stalks?

SLUGS AND SNAILS

Is it a fine web?

VINE WEEVIL

Is the compost very wet?

see: LEAFDROP

Is there yellow or silvery mottling?

Is it a grey, furry growth?

Is it a fine, white, powdery coating?

ROOT ROT

RED SPIDER MITE

GREY MOULD

POWDERY MILDEW

Do they look like a network of small tunnels?

WHOLE PLANT

LEAF MINER

Is the plant wilting or collapsed?

Is it a tomato plant?

Are there white grubs in the soil?

FOOT ROT

Is the compost very wet?

Are there clouds of flies when the plant is disturbed?

ROOT ROT

VINE WEEVIL (larvae)

Are the flies white?

Are they black?

Are the fruits of tomatoes/peppers dark and hardened at one end?

WHITEFLY

FUNGUS GNATS

BLOSSOM END ROT

Pests & Diseases
Pests

It is important to have an idea of the pests and diseases that could affect your plants grown under glass, and this short guide will give you some idea of the most common and how they can best be dealt with.

Aphids

Aphids are small insects that feed on sap. They stunt growth by removing sap from the growing points and this can lead to a distortion of leaves and tips as they grow. After sucking sap they excrete some of it and this can cause sooty mould to develop. They also transmit viruses from plant to plant. The best way of controlling aphids is to spot them early. They reproduce at an incredible rate, so squashing one early on in the season has a huge effect. Examine plants every few days, and kill all the aphids you see. If you get a large infestation, there are sprays that will kill them. Try mixing a mild solution of soapy water – a tiny drop of washing up liquid in a bottle of water – and use a sprayer to target the aphids. The soap clogs up their pores and they die. Check and repeat as necessary.

Mealybugs

These are small, soft-bodied insects that are covered in a waxy, white coating. They suck sap from plants and are hard to remove, partly because they attack parts of plants that are difficult to reach, and partly because their coating repels sprays. Inspect plants regularly. If left untreated they can distort growing tips and cause sooty mould and eventually weaken a plant. Remove them with a cotton bud or paintbrush. Dip the tip of the brush or cotton bud in methylated spirits, as this wipes off the waxy coating, making them easier to remove. Try not to damage the plant with the methylated spirits.

Scale insects

Scale insects are similar to mealybugs, in that they are sap suckers and are fairly immobile. They stay in one spot and put their mouth parts into the plant to extract sap. They distort growth, weaken the plant and excrete honeydew, which leads to the development of sooty mould. As they are generally immobile, however, you are most likely to get a problem by bringing an infested plant into your home, so carefully check over any new plants. Scale can be wiped off with a soft cloth or with a cotton bud. They do not usually need to be wiped with methylated spirits, as with mealybugs, but if they prove difficult to remove, use a mild soap solution.

Leaf miner

Leaf miner is a pest of chrysanthemums. The affected leaves look as if a network of small, winding tunnels have been dug just under the surface. The patches of leaf in between these tunnels can then turn pale or yellow. This is not a particularly serious pest and, unless the infestation is severe, simply remove and burn any affected leaves. If it becomes necessary, treat with an insecticide.

Scale insects

Slugs and snails are less of a problem in a greenhouse or conservatory situation than they are out of doors, but they are worth looking out for as they can cause devastating damage to leaves and stems. They are particularly damaging to young seedlings as they can strip leaves and effectively kill these young plants. You are unlikely to have problems with them in a conservatory, but a greenhouse is more vulnerable. Keeping susceptible plants on benches will help, but the best way to beat them is simply to keep your eyes open and check your greenhouse regularly. Slugs and snails often lurk on the moist bottoms of pots and seed trays to emerge at night, so check these areas regularly. Use slug pellets only in cases of severe infestation.

Fungus gnats

Fungus gnats do not usually cause great harm, but should be contained as they become more troublesome as their numbers increase. Adults are usually seen flying above the compost of potted plants. They need moist soil in which to lay their eggs and occur most often over winter on plants that have been overwatered and left with soggy soil. They also prefer fresh compost that is high in organic matter to older compost. Do not overwater plants in winter and do not re-pot or top-dress with fresh compost until spring. Once you have an infestation, it is possible to stop the adults laying more eggs by letting the soil dry out. However, this can make the problem slightly worse as the larvae that have hatched in the soil will turn on the roots as the nearest available source of moisture. Try sprinkling the surface of the pot with fine sand. As this dries out more quickly than compost, it can fool the adults into thinking that the compost is dry and this can break the cycle.

Red spider mites

This is a serious, sap-sucking pest that can severely weaken plants. Red spider mites are tiny red, green or yellow mites that are almost invisible to the naked eye – you will see them better by looking through a magnifying glass. You are more likely to notice the symptoms of an infestation than to notice the pest itself. The first sign is usually a yellow mottling of the leaf or the appearance of small, yellow patches. As an infestation develops, a fine web starts to appear over the leaves and stems. The good news is that red spider mites rarely attack healthy, vigorous plants. They prefer to go for plants that are already weakened in some way, perhaps plants that have not been potted on for a long time or that are suffering from drought. Red spider mites love dry conditions and an attack is usually the result of low humidity around a susceptible plant. Make sure you keep the humidity high around plants that need it and this pest is unlikely to cause a problem. Raise the humidity around infested plants to try to control the pest, but throw away those with severe infestations or the pest will spread to other plants.

Thrips

Thrips are a pest of flowers. They attack petals and flowerbuds, causing silvering and mottling, and sometimes distortion of the flower as it grows. Thrips may also deposit small red and brown droplets on the flowers. The thrips themselves are extremely small and have dark brown and yellow bodies. It is more usual to notice the symptoms rather than the pest itself. Thrips only usually attack plants that are under stress. The usual conditions under which they occur are in hot, dry conditions, so move infested plants to a cooler, more humid situation. Try to prevent infestations by keeping plants in the correct growing conditions and by watering them regularly. If they continue to be a problem it is possible to buy contact insecticides.

Vine weevil

Adult vine weevils can chomp through leaves, but it is their larvae that cause the real problem. Adults lay them in the compost and when they hatch they start eating through the roots. Adults leave their characteristic notches in the leaves, however, often there will be no outward sign and the first you know of a problem is when your plant collapses. It is almost impossible to save them when they have reached this point. If you do spot an infestation before it is too late, there is a vine weevil killer, which you can apply to the soil.

Whitefly

Whiteflies are sap-sucking insects that feed on the lower sides of leaves causing leaf distortion. Clouds of the small white flies will fly up into the air when the plant is disturbed. Adults lay their eggs on the lower side of the leaf. A bad infestation can weaken a plant. There are several ways of controlling whiteflies without having to resort to chemicals. Because the adults fly around the plant, a sticky trap placed close to an infested plant will kill quite a large number of them. You can also mix up a mild soap solution – a tiny drop of washing up liquid mixed in a bottle of water is excellent – and use a mister to spray it over adults and the eggs.

Diseases

Grey mould

Grey mould is most often a problem of flowering plants, as it starts in flowers and buds. However, it can also affect some foliage plants. It is a velvety, grey-brown fungal growth, often found on plants that are being kept in cold and damp conditions. Overwatering plants will make them more susceptible. Flowers that have gone over but have not been removed from the plant are an ideal breeding ground for the fungus, as are over-ripe fruits and dead or damaged leaves and stems. Always deadhead flowers as they die, and remove any dead or damaged plant tissue as soon as you spot it. If plants are affected, remove all diseased parts and move the plants into lighter, warmer conditions with good ventilation. As with many diseases of indoor plants, grey mould is unlikely to get a hold if the plant is healthy and is actively growing.

Powdery mildew

Powdery mildew can be a serious disease on some indoor plants. It starts as small white patches and gradually spreads to become a light, powdery coating over leaves and stems. In severe cases, leaves can turn yellow and drop, and the whole plant may collapse. Powdery mildew usually becomes a problem in hot and dry environments, so make sure plants are shaded from hot sun and do not suffer from drought. It is also a problem where plants are placed close together and do not receive enough air. Space plants out and ensure good ventilation. Try cutting out and burning or throwing away the affected parts, however this can shake the fungal spores onto lower foliage and cause further problems.

Rust

Rusts can be a problem on many indoor plants, particularly chrysanthemums, Cineraria and pelargoniums. It usually appears as brown blisters on surfaces or undersides of the leaves. As blisters develop, they can turn various colours including yellow and black. They gradually spread and the plant goes slowly into decline, and starts losing leaves. Less flowers are formed and the plant will eventually die. The best prevention is to take care when watering. If water is allowed to sit on the leaves, plants are more likely to suffer from rusts. Remove infected foliage and burn it or throw it away.

Sooty mould

Sooty mould appears as a brown or black soot-like covering to the leaves. It is usually associated with sap-feeding insects, such as aphids or mealybugs. As these pests feed on the leaves, they excrete a sugary substance called honeydew. This lands on the leaves below, and fungi move in and feed on the honeydew. Although the fungus does not attack the plants, it is important that it is controlled as it cuts down on the light available to the leaves and can weaken plants or at least stop them from growing at their usual rate. To treat sooty mould, first treat for the insect infestation. Once that is dealt with, carefully sponge off the mould.

Oedema

Oedema is a common, but not particularly serious, problem in pelargoniums. It can also often be seen in cacti, Peperomia and begonias. Small, warty growths appear on the stems and undersides of leaves of plants. The texture of the leaf may also become rough. Oedema is usually caused by overwatering and too high humidity, leading to the plant taking up excess water. The warts do not cause any problems other than looking unusual. Avoid overwatering. Improved ventilation can also help to prevent the problem.

Virus

There are many different viruses that can affect indoor plants such as hyacinths, Narcissus, begonias, figs, orchids, chrysanthemums, pelargoniums and Cyclamen. Plants can be infected and not show any symptoms for a long time. In these cases, the virus simply results in a gradual decline in the plant's health. Classic symptoms to look for include mottled, puckered or streaked foliage and distorted, deformed or strangely coloured flowers. Viruses are often spread by aphids, so good aphid control can prevent infection. They are also spread by gardeners, so be sure to clean secateurs and other equipment after taking cuttings. Once plants are infected, there is no treatment. Throw the plant away or burn it.

Brown tips

Many plants will gradually get brown tips as they age. Fresh young foliage emerges a healthy green, and over time leaf edges and tips appear to dry out and turn brown. The cause is most often due to underwatering and low humidity. Other causes can include physical damage, where the plant is being brushed against on a regular basis. Move them to a more protected spot. If brown tips are associated with yellowing of the leaves, there can be other causes, including overwatering, draughts, too high or low light levels and lack of food.

Leaf drop

A sudden loss of leaves on a favourite plant can be distressing. It can be due to a number of factors, and you will need to look at the plant's environment to determine the problem. Plants that have just been brought into the home can suddenly drop leaves. This will be the change in environment and can also occur when moving a plant within the home. It is quite likely that a newly bought plant has come from the extremely light and warm environment of a glasshouse into the relative darkness of the home. Move it to a slightly lighter spot for a few days. Try to move established indoor plants as little as possible. Other causes include draughts and sudden changes in light levels or temperatures. Both underwatering and overwatering can cause leaf drop.

Root rot

Problems with overwatered plants are only usually noticed when the plant starts to die. In winter it is easy to overwater plants and the first signs of overwatering can look similar to drought, as the plant starts to droop. Many people then make the problem worse by adding more water and this prevents air from reaching the roots, which can then start to rot. If plants show the first signs of overwatering in winter, pull the root ball out of the pot and inspect it. Overwatered roots will be completely sodden. Allow air to get to the roots by keeping the rootball out of the pot and placing it on top of the upturned pot for a few days while it dries out.

Blossom end rot

This is a problem that is only usually found in tomatoes and peppers. The base of the developing fruit gradually turns dark in colour and becomes hardened. This area will gradually shrink and causes the fruit to become malformed. It is associated with calcium deficiency most often caused by a lack of water. If plants are kept well-watered throughout the growing season it should not occur.

Foot rot

Foot rot is sometimes seen in tomatoes. Leaves seem small and yellow, and may wilt. Black areas or spots may appear near the base of the stem. Foot rot is caused by a fungus and is most common on tomato plants that are being grown where previous tomato crops have been recently grown. This is why it is essential not to grow tomatoes, or any other annual crops, in greenhouse borders, but instead to use grow bags or pots of fresh soil. Foot rot can also be caused by water from water butts that has been left to sit for a long period.

Index

Acknowledgements

The publishers would like to thank Coolings Nurseries for their cooperation and assistance with the photography in this book, including the loan of tools and much specialist equipment. Special thanks go to: Sandra Gratwick. Coolings Nurseries Ltd., Rushmore Hill, Knockholt, Kent, TN14 7NN. Tel: 00 44 1959 532269; Email: coolings@coolings.co.uk; Website: www.coolings.co.uk.